ENGLISH

KnowHow

Student Book 2

Therese Naber · **Angela Blackwell**

with Gregory J. Manin

OXFORD

UNIVERSITY PRESS

Contents

Contents

Listening / Speaking	Reading / Writing	*KnowHow*
➤ Listening: • A story about a lottery ticket • An interview about bartering ➤ Speaking: • Sayings about money • Finding people to barter with • Solving treasure-hunting clues	➤ Reading: • *The Gift* • *Treasure in the City* ➤ Writing: • Barter notices • Treasure-hunting clues	➤ Dealing with mistakes
➤ Listening: • Making potato chips • A folk tale about salt ➤ Speaking: • A food history quiz • Presenting a cooking show script • Discussing local products	➤ Reading: *Ostrich Mania* ➤ Writing: • A cooking show script • A publicity brochure about local products	➤ Consonant clusters
➤ Listening: • Song – "On the Road Again" • Personal travel stories • A modern explorer ➤ Speaking: • Discussing views on traveling • Creating an advertisement for a trip	➤ Reading: • A book review and extract from *8 Men and a Duck* ➤ Writing: A personal travel story	➤ Improving fluency
➤ Listening: • News story about sports and superstitions • Song – "Do You Believe in Magic" • Stories of first impressions ➤ Speaking: • Identifying superstitions • Discussing first impressions	➤ Reading: *Reading Faces* ➤ Writing: • Your own superstitions • Personal stories of first impressions	➤ Common vowel sounds
➤ Listening: • Health benefits of nature • Animal intelligence ➤ Speaking: • Comparing landscapes • Choosing an appropriate pet	➤ Reading: An article about an oceanographer ➤ Writing: A story about a special characteristic of an animal	➤ Choosing vocabulary to learn
➤ Listening: A radio call-in show ➤ Speaking: "The *If…* Game"	➤ Reading: • Extract: *Dear Jean: What They Don't Teach You at the Water Cooler* • *Social Customs…* ➤Writing: Asking for and giving advice	➤ Intonation patterns

1 All work and no play

✔ Work and leisure
✔ *So / neither*; gerunds and infinitives

1 Reading

a Look at the photographs. What are the people doing in each one?

b Read the article. Which answer is the most unusual?

How do you RELAX?
What do you do to UNWIND?

Andrew: I love to sit on my steps with a cup of coffee and watch the world go by. It's so relaxing at the end of a long day or after doing chores. I watch the neighborhood children play and it helps me unwind and forget my worries.

Charlotte: Playing the guitar is always relaxing for me. Most days I sit down and play a little after work. I also get together with friends who play instruments a few times a week. We play together and chat about things.

Nathan: After work on Friday evenings, a lot of people get together to make "slushies" from the cleanest snow on earth. We put fresh snow in a glass and add our favorite drink flavors to the snow. The slushies are great, but really it's just an excuse for people to socialize and discuss the week. It's a great way to take it easy and socialize at the same time.

c Read the article again. Who relaxes alone? Who gets together with other people?

2 Vocabulary: Work and leisure

a Discuss these expressions. Which relate more to work? Which relate more to leisure?

unwind   have a long / hard day   get together (with friends)   be by yourself   take it easy
forget your worries   do chores   get away (for a while)   socialize   work hard

b Work in groups and answer the questions. Report the answers to the class.

1 How do you unwind after a hard day?
2 Is it usually easy for you to forget your worries?
3 Do you like to get away for a while?
4 Do you enjoy being by yourself?

3 Focus on Grammar

a AUDIO Listen to the conversations based on the chart. Circle the last response you hear in each conversation. Is the person agreeing or disagreeing? Then answer questions 1 and 2.

1 Which auxiliary verbs are used with the following verb tenses?
   present continuous   simple present and past   present perfect simple

2 What is the order of the subject and auxiliary with *so* and *neither*?

Review of auxiliary verbs; Responding with *so* and *neither*			
Question		**Agreeing**	**Disagreeing**
Present continuous			
Are you relaxing today?	Yes, I **am**.	So **am** I.	I'm not.
Simple present			
Do you enjoy being by yourself?	Yes, I **do**.	So **do** I.	I **don't**.
Simple past			
Did you work yesterday?	No, I **didn't**.	**Neither did** I.	I **did**.
Present perfect simple			
Have you finished your work?	No, I **haven't**.	**Neither have** I.	I **have**.

b AUDIO Complete the conversations with a form of *do*, *be*, or *have*. Listen and check.

1 A: ᵃ *Do* ____ you like to ski a lot?
   B: Yes, I ᵇ____.
   A: So ᶜ____ I.

2 A: What ᵃ____ you doing?
   B: I ᵇ____ relaxing. I had a hard day.
   A: So ᶜ____ I!

3 A: ᵃ____ you go out last night?
   B: No, I ᵇ____.
   A: I ᶜ____. I had a good time.

4 A: ᵃ____ you ever been to Scotland?
   B: No, I ᵇ____.
   A: Neither ᶜ____ I, but I'd like to go.

c Work with a partner. Practice the conversations in 3b using information that is true for you.

Example   A: *Have you ever been to Florida?*
          B: *No, I haven't. Have you?*
          A: *Yes, I have. I went last year.*

4 Listening

a What topics do people often talk about when they meet for the first time?

b AUDIO Listen. Number these topics in the order you hear them.

a walking   __   c jobs   __
b where they live __   d the conference   __

c AUDIO Listen again. Check the correct box for each piece of information.

	Jessica	Adam	Both
1 usually walk(s) outside			
2 live(s) in Canada			
3 like(s) the outdoors			
4 live(s) near Phoenix			
5 work(s) in sales			

2

5 Language in Action: Making conversation

a **AUDIO** Look at the conversational expressions in the chart. Listen to the conversation in 4b again. Check the expressions Adam and Jessica use.

INTRODUCING A TOPIC	ASKING FOLLOW-UP QUESTIONS	ENDING A CONVERSATION
__ Where do you live?	__ What's (place name) like?	__ It was nice to meet you.
__ Where are you from?	__ Where exactly is (place name)?	__ It was nice talking to you.
__ What do you do?	__ Tell me about….	__ I'll see you (tomorrow).
__ What do you do in your free time?	__ What about you?	

b **AUDIO** Fill in the blanks with an expression from the chart above. Listen and check your answers. Then use real information and practice the conversations with a partner.

1 **A:** *What do you do?*
   B: I'm a graphic designer.
   _____?
   A: I'm a computer programmer.

2 **A:** _____?
   B: I like scuba diving.
   A: Oh, so do I!

3 **A:** _____?
   B: In Mexico City.
   A: _____?
   B: It's beautiful.

4 **A:** _____.
   B: Nice to meet you, too.

6 Speaking

a Try to think of one or two questions for each topic below. Look at section 5 to help you.

   1 job   2 where you live   3 family   4 leisure activities

b Imagine you are at a conference. Use your own name and personal information (or invent new information). Mingle and make conversations with other people. Use expressions from section 5 and questions from 6a. Try to keep the conversations going!

7 Reading

a Look at the picture of Nathan Tift, who works at the South Pole. What questions would you want to ask him?

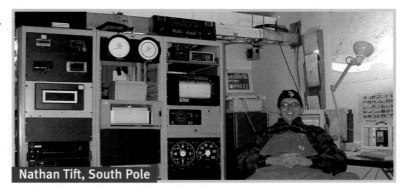

Nathan Tift, South Pole

b Read the questions. Are any the same as your questions in 7a? Then read the article. Fill in the blanks with the questions.

What do you do for fun there?   Do you mind the nonstop sunlight or darkness?
What time zone are you in?   What are your living conditions like?
What's your job there?   How long are you going to be there?
                                 How many people live and work there?

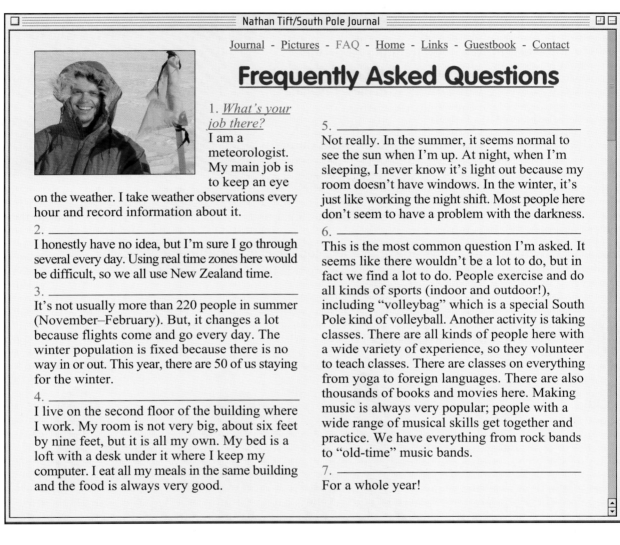

Nathan Tift/South Pole Journal

Journal - Pictures - FAQ - Home - Links - Guestbook - Contact

Frequently Asked Questions

1. *What's your job there?*
I am a meteorologist. My main job is to keep an eye on the weather. I take weather observations every hour and record information about it.

2. _____
I honestly have no idea, but I'm sure I go through several every day. Using real time zones here would be difficult, so we all use New Zealand time.

3. _____
It's not usually more than 220 people in summer (November–February). But, it changes a lot because flights come and go every day. The winter population is fixed because there is no way in or out. This year, there are 50 of us staying for the winter.

4. _____
I live on the second floor of the building where I work. My room is not very big, about six feet by nine feet, but it is all my own. My bed is a loft with a desk under it where I keep my computer. I eat all my meals in the same building and the food is always very good.

5. _____
Not really. In the summer, it seems normal to see the sun when I'm up. At night, when I'm sleeping, I never know it's light out because my room doesn't have windows. In the winter, it's just like working the night shift. Most people here don't seem to have a problem with the darkness.

6. _____
This is the most common question I'm asked. It seems like there wouldn't be a lot to do, but in fact we find a lot to do. People exercise and do all kinds of sports (indoor and outdoor!), including "volleybag" which is a special South Pole kind of volleyball. Another activity is taking classes. There are all kinds of people here with a wide variety of experience, so they volunteer to teach classes. There are classes on everything from yoga to foreign languages. There are also thousands of books and movies here. Making music is always very popular; people with a wide range of musical skills get together and practice. We have everything from rock bands to "old-time" music bands.

7. _____
For a whole year!

c Read the article again. Write T (true), F (false), or NI (no information). Give reasons for your answers.

1 Nathan checks the weather regularly for his job.   ___
2 He always knows which time zone he is in.   ___
3 The population in winter changes a lot.   ___
4 He lives, works, and eats in the same building.   ___
5 He is a very good cook.   ___
6 People only do indoor activities at the South Pole.   ___
7 He watches a lot of foreign movies.   ___

d What do you think about Nathan Tift's life? How would you feel about living at the South Pole?

8 ▶ In Conversation

AUDIO Do the friends agree on the chores they like and dislike? Listen. Then read.

Holly: That was delicious, Scott.

All: Yes, it was. Really good.

Scott: Thank you.

Rob: You really enjoy cooking, don't you?

Scott: Yes, I do. It's not a chore for me at all. In fact, I enjoy it! But I hate doing the dishes. I never want to do the dishes.

Marie: I'm the opposite. I can't stand cooking, but I don't mind doing the dishes.

Rob: The chore I really hate is ironing. Ugh!

Holly: Oh, I don't mind ironing at all. I usually plan to watch TV at the same time. It's not so bad.

Scott: It's funny how different people feel about different chores.

Holly: Yes, but no one likes taking out the garbage, right?

All: Not me! I don't!

9 ▶ Vocabulary: Chores

a Match 1–7 with a–g to describe chores.

1	wash	_1d_	a	bills
2	do	—	b	the garbage
3	take out	—	c	the rug or the carpet
4	mop / sweep	—	d	windows or the car
5	pay	—	e	laundry or the dishes or yard work
6	iron	—	f	the floor
7	vacuum	—	g	clothes

b Which chores do you do regularly? Which do you never do?

10 ▶ Focus on Grammar

a Look at the chart. Find other examples of verbs with gerunds and infinitives in the conversation on page 5.

Gerunds and infinitives
Verb + gerund (-ing)
I **enjoy cooking.**   *enjoy, don't mind, can't stand* I **don't mind doing** the dishes.
Verb + infinitive (to + base form)
I don't **want to do** the dishes.   *want, plan, need, would like, hope* I don't **need to wash** the car.
Note: You can use the infinitive or the gerund with *like, love,* and *hate.* *I like doing chores.* OR *I like to do chores.*

b Fill in the blanks with the correct form of the verb in parentheses. More than one answer is possible in two sentences.

1 Alan enjoys _____*washing*_____ (wash) the car.
2 Do you mind _____ (do) chores?
3 We hope _____ (finish) our work this afternoon.
4 Kyoko doesn't like _____ (take) out the garbage.
5 It's a nice day, so they want _____ (wash) the windows.
6 What are they planning _____ (do) tomorrow?
7 The children love _____ (play) in the park.
8 Would you like _____ (go) out for dinner tonight?

> ▼ **Help Desk**
>
> Use *like* to say that you enjoy (doing) something good.
> *I **like** cooking.*
>
> Use *would like* as a polite way of saying that you want (to do) something.
> *I'd **like** to cook dinner tonight.*

c Write sentences about yourself. Then compare sentences with a partner.

Example   *I enjoy swimming and going out with friends.*

1 I enjoy _____.
2 I don't mind _____.
3 I can't stand _____.
4 I love _____.
5 Next weekend, I plan _____.
6 Someday, I'd like _____.
7 Next year, I want _____.
8 After class, I need _____.

Listening

a Read the cartoon. What feelings does it express about being a child?

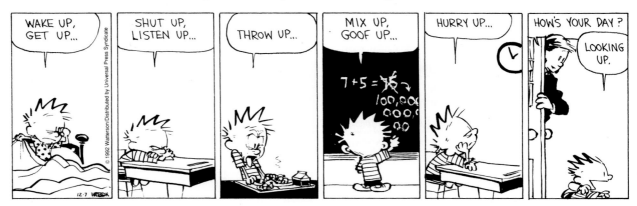

b AUDIO Listen. Write one positive and one negative thing that each child mentions.

	Positive	Negative
1	*play a lot*	
2		
3		

c AUDIO Listen again. Check the topics each child talks about.

	1	2	3
sports and games	✓		
friends			
homework and school			
chores			
adults and work			
birthdays and presents			
food			
paying for things			

12 ▸ Speaking

a What are two positive points and two negative points of each of these stages of life? Make notes of your ideas.

    child   teenager   adult

    Example *A good thing about being a child is that you don't have to pay taxes.*

b Compare answers in groups or as a class. Are there points that are the same at any stage of life? Which stage of life has the most positive points?

13 ▸ Writing

a Choose one stage of life. Write a paragraph summarizing the positive and negative points.

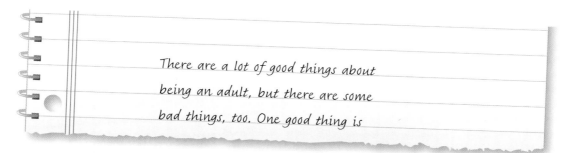

There are a lot of good things about being an adult, but there are some bad things, too. One good thing is

b Work in groups. Read other students' paragraphs. Which stage had the most positive points in your group? Why?

14 ▸ *KnowHow*: Learning tips

a Work with a partner. Discuss the questions about learning English.

1. Why are you studying English?
2. Which areas are the most difficult for you? Which are the easiest?
3. What do you enjoy about learning English?
4. What do you want to improve in English?

b Work in small groups. Discuss these areas of language learning. What strategies make a successful learner? Try to add at least one more idea to each category.

Grammar	Vocabulary	Speaking	Listening	Reading	Writing
Make notes with helpful information.	Review a lot.	Practice as much as you can.	Don't worry if you don't understand every word.	Think about the topic before you start.	Make notes before you start.

c Work as a class. Make a master list of your strategies for successful language learning.

2 Making sense

✔ Language and the senses
✔ Uses of the present continuous; stative verbs

1 ▶ Reading

a Read the messages below. Can you match the messages in bold with these expressions?

see you   got to go   hold on   What's up?   talk to you later

sup Danny?

Instant Message
File Edit Insert

Nothing. **h/o** Lena's calling. She wants to meet after work. OK?

A **A** A A B *I* u ☺ Send

OK. **g2g.** My meeting's starting! **ttyl**

Instant Message
File Edit Insert

c ya

b Read the article. What are the two different opinions on language change?

c Read the article again and answer the questions.

1 What do these abbreviations mean: *ILB L8*, *FYI*, and *IMO*?
2 What is the possible confusion about the abbreviation *LOL*?

d What do you think? Discuss these questions in small groups.

1 Think of words or expressions that are "new" in your language. Where do they come from?
2 Do you think your language is changing? Give examples, if possible.

Text messaging: New language or not?

YOU'RE SITTING ON A BUS, rushing to meet a friend and you're late. So, you get out your cell phone and type "ILB L8" ("I'll be late") and press "send."

Text messaging is clearly affecting language. There are no rules to it, and the language is constantly evolving. We are composing a new aspect of vocabulary and opening up a new kind of playful, direct, and 24-hour communication.

And, what is happening to good old-fashioned English? Dr. Ken Lodge, a linguistics expert, says, "Text messaging is fun and that's fine, but I'm worried about the effects it might have on a child's ability to read and write."

Not everyone is so worried. Language professor Jean Aitchison says, "Every time a new medium comes along it has an effect on language…. But this doesn't destroy the existing language, it adds to it and embellishes it."

In text messages, many words come from shorthand created in e-mail, such as FYI (for your information) and IMO (in my opinion). Aitchison says, "Mostly they are original, but sometimes you get a clash of meanings. For example, take LOL, which can mean both Laugh Out Loud and Lots of Love. That could lead to some embarrassing misunderstandings."

2 ▶ Focus on Grammar

a Review the uses of the present continuous in sentences 1–4. Which sentences describe actions happening <u>right now</u>? Which describe actions happening <u>around now</u>?

1 The phone is ringing. Can you answer it?
2 He's studying French this year.
3 We're working on a new project this month.
4 It's raining, so take an umbrella.

b Look at the chart. Find at least two examples of the present continuous for changing or developing situations in the article on page 9.

More uses of the present continuous

For changing or developing situations.
Language is changing all the time.   The weather is getting warmer these days.
For arrangements and plans in the future, usually when time and place are decided.
They're leaving for Madrid next Monday.   Elise is having a party on Friday at 9:00 p.m.

---

c Write two sentences with the present continuous for each situation. Then compare answers with a partner.

1 Something you're doing right now:
  Right now, I'm writing in my notebook .
  Right now, _____ .
2 Something you're doing around now, but not right now:
  This week, _____ .
  This month, _____ .

3 A situation that is changing or developing:
  The weather is _____ .
  These days, _____ .
4 Something you're doing in the future:
  Tomorrow, _____ .
  Next week, _____ .

3 ▶ Vocabulary: Expressions with *get*

a Look at the different uses of *get* in these expressions. Put each expression into the correct diagram.

get better   get home   get a letter   get there   get some new clothes   get angry

b Fill in the blanks with the correct form of these expressions.

get a newspaper   get hungry   get a taxi
get bigger   get here   get new clothes

1 Let's have dinner. I'm *getting hungry.*
2 Gina went shopping to _____ .
3 The children are _____ every day.
4 I didn't know you were here. What time did you _____ ?
5 We need to _____ . We don't have time to walk.
6 Chris _____ every morning at the newsstand.

become	get dark, get worse, get bigger, get hungry, _____, _____
obtain OR receive	get a job, get a newspaper, get a taxi, _____, _____
arrive	get back, get here, _____, _____

4 ▸ Listening

a Look at the words and expressions. Which ones do you recognize?

> curiosity   fabulous   flabbergasted   forward
> happiness   hectic   imagination   strength
> "Curiosity killed the cat."   "come easy"

b **AUDIO** Listen to people talking about their favorite words and expressions. Write the words or expressions in the chart after the correct name.

He's flabbergasted.   It's a hectic day.

	Word / expression	Reason
Silvia	hectic, forward	
Victor	_____	
Fabiana	_____	
Takahiro	_____	
Anna	_____ , _____ , _____	
Alfredo	_____ , _____	

c **AUDIO** Listen again. Complete the chart with the reasons the people give for their answers.

d Which of these words do you like best? Why?

5 ▸ Vocabulary: Word building (noun suffixes)

a Look at the examples. What are four suffixes used to make a verb or adjective into a noun? What spelling changes do you notice?

> happy—happiness   curious—curiosity   excite—excitement   imagine—imagination

b Write the noun forms of these verbs and adjectives in the correct category. (Use the numbers to choose the correct category.)

> creative (2)   achieve (3)   kind (1)   educate (4)   manage (3)   dark (1)
> explore (4)   stupid (2)   good (1)   govern (3)   sleepy (1)   sad (1)
> celebrate (4)   similar (2)   translate (4)   possible (2)

(1) -ness	(2) -ity	(3) -ment	(4) -ation
happiness	curiosity	excitement	imagination
	creativity	achievement	

c Fill in the blanks with the noun forms of the words in bold.

1 Let's **celebrate**. / Let's have a _celebration_.
2 Children are often very **curious**. / Children often have a lot of _____.
3 It's **possible** we will finish the project today. / There is a _____ we will finish today.
4 The two pictures are very **similar**. / There is a lot of _____ between the two pictures.
5 Good artists are usually very **creative**. / Good artists usually have a lot of _____.
6 They work hard and **achieve** a lot. / They have many _____.

6 KnowHow: Word stress

a **AUDIO** Listen to the stress on these words. Where is the stress for words that end in *-ity*? For words that end in *-ation*?

creative—creativity curious—curiosity imagine—imagination celebrate—celebration

b **AUDIO** Mark the stress and practice saying these words. Then listen and check.

exploration   similarity   possibility   translation   education   stupidity

c List three more words with these endings. Practice the words with a partner.

7 Language in Action: Talking about language

a **AUDIO** Listen. What word are Victor and Silvia talking about?

b **AUDIO** Listen again. Check the questions Victor asks Silvia.

LANGUAGE QUESTIONS
___ What does this word mean?
___ What does (flabbergasted) mean?
___ How do you say it?
___ How do you pronounce it?
___ How many syllables does it have?
___ Is it a (noun / verb…)?
___ What kind of word is it?
___ Is it a formal / informal word?

c Work with a partner. Use words from sections 4 and 5 to make your own conversations.

Example A: *What does* hectic *mean?*
            B: *I'm not sure, but I think it means "very busy."*

8 Speaking

a Work in groups. Ask and answer questions about your favorite words and expressions. Write each person's favorite word(s) in English and the reasons.

b Make a list of favorite words as a class. Did some people choose the same word? Did you learn any new words?

Name	Word(s)	Reasons

9 ▶ Reading

a Match each verb (1–5) to the part of the body (a–e) it is usually associated with.

1	taste	*1d*	a	ears
2	smell	—	b	fingers
3	see / look (at)	—	c	nose
4	hear / listen (to)	—	d	mouth
5	feel / touch	—	e	eyes

b Read the article. What is synesthesia? Do all people who experience synesthesia describe it the same way?

S Y N E S T H E S I A

While most of us experience the world through orderly senses, for some people, two or more senses mix together. This phenomenon is called *synesthesia*.

People with synesthesia often see letters and words as colored. They also may feel or taste sounds or hear or taste shapes: a musical note that tastes like pickles, a taste of chicken that feels "round," or the sound of a guitar that feels like a soft touch on a person's leg.

One aspect of the phenomenon is that different people do not have the same experience. For example, letters do not produce the same color for everyone. Carol Steen says that the letter *L* is black with blue highlights, but her friend Patricia Duffy, who also has synesthesia, says *L* is pale yellow.

People with synesthesia have described their symptoms for more than 200 years; at times synesthesia was viewed as an illness, while at other times people who experienced it were seen as artistically gifted. Often, they were simply not believed at all.

It was only by the end of the twentieth century that researchers were able to identify and record the variety of these sensations. They say that synesthesia seems to run in families—the Russian novelist Vladimir Nabokov, his mother, and his son all experienced it. It is more common in women than men, and it is an international phenomenon. Beyond this, there are still many aspects of synesthesia that are not understood. For example, scientists are not even sure how many people experience it. Neuroscientist Peter Grossenbacher says, "We understand it's a real experience. But we don't know yet how it comes to pass."

c Read the article again. Explain the following.

1 Two ways someone with synesthesia might experience music: _____
2 One thing that Carol Steen and Patricia Duffy disagree about: _____
3 Three ways people in the past viewed synesthesia: _____
4 Two things that scientists know about synesthesia: _____

d Find the words and expressions (1–7) in the article on page 13. Match them with the correct definitions (a–g). (1) = paragraph number.

1 orderly (1)　　　　　　_1b_　　a happen
2 phenomenon (1)　　　___　　b well-arranged, well-organized
3 symptoms (4)　　　　 ___　　c feelings in the body or mind
4 gifted (4)　　　　　　 ___　　d something (often unusual) that happens or exists
5 sensations (5)　　　　 ___　　e be typical, happen often
6 run in (families) (5)　 ___　　f having natural ability or great intelligence
7 come to pass (6)　　　 ___　　g signs that something is wrong or different than it
　　　　　　　　　　　　　　　　　normally is

e Have you ever known or heard of anyone who experiences synesthesia?

10 ▸ Listening

a Look at the illustration of a person's experience of synesthesia. What do you think this person's experience is related to?

b **AUDIO** Listen. Check your guess above and answer these questions.

1 When did she experience synesthesia?　　2 How does she feel about it?

c **AUDIO** Listen again. Put the following words under the correct day of the week.

**ballet teacher　clouds　rectangle　bright yellow　brown　gray
velvet curtain　orange　a stage　red (x2)　lilac　blue**

Monday	Tuesday	Wednesday	Thursday	Friday	Saturday	Sunday
		ballet teacher				

d What do you think it would be like to experience synesthesia?

Focus on Grammar

a Look at the chart. Based on the chart, which of the following words are stative verbs?

understand   run   need   speak   sweep   love   write   wash   eat   sound

---

Stative (non-action) verbs

- **Descriptions and the senses:** *be, hear, look, see, seem, smell, sound, taste*
  Louise seems happy.

- **Possessions:** *have, own*
  Carlos has a new car.

- **Emotions and attitudes:** *like, love, hate, want, need*
  They like music.

- **Ideas:** *think, understand, know, believe*
  We know the answer.

Note: Stative verbs are not usually used in the continuous. But some of these verbs (*look, feel, taste, smell, have,* and *think*) can also be action verbs and use a continuous form.

Stative	That book **looks** interesting.	I **have** a new car.
Action	I'm **looking** at this book because I want to buy it.	I'm **having** problems with my car.

---

b Find four examples of stative verbs in the article on page 13.

c Complete the conversations with the simple present or present continuous of the verb in parentheses.

1 A: What ª *are you doing* (you / do)?
   B: I ᵇ_____ (smell) the flowers. They ᶜ_____ (smell) wonderful!
2 A: What's that noise? It ª_____ (sound) awful.
   B: It's James. He ᵇ_____ (practice) the trumpet.
   A: Oh, sorry. I ᶜ_____ (think) he needs more practice.
3 A: You ª_____ (seem) unhappy. What's the matter?
   B: I ᵇ_____ (not / like) my job. I ᶜ_____ (have) too much work.
   A: That's too bad. ᵈ_____ (you / look) for another one?
4 A: What's the matter?
   B: I ª_____ (do) my homework, but I ᵇ_____ (not / understand) this math.
   A: ᶜ_____ (you / need) help?
5 A: You ª_____ (look) tired.
   B: I am. I ᵇ_____ (have) a terrible cold, too.
   A: Have you taken anything for it?
   B: Yes, and it ᶜ_____ (get) a little better.

d Use these ideas (or your own) and make true sentences. Then compare answers with a partner.

I		be	look		good / bad
You		seem	have		tall / short
My brother / sister	**+**	feel	like	**+**	blond hair / brown eyes
A lot of people		understand			Italian / history / math
My friend					a new job / a car
					tired / sick

Examples *My sister has brown eyes.*
          You seem tired today.

12 ▶ Speaking

a Look at the questionnaire. Make notes of your answers. Then work in pairs and interview your partner.

b Work in small groups. Present your partner's answers to the group. Are any answers the same?

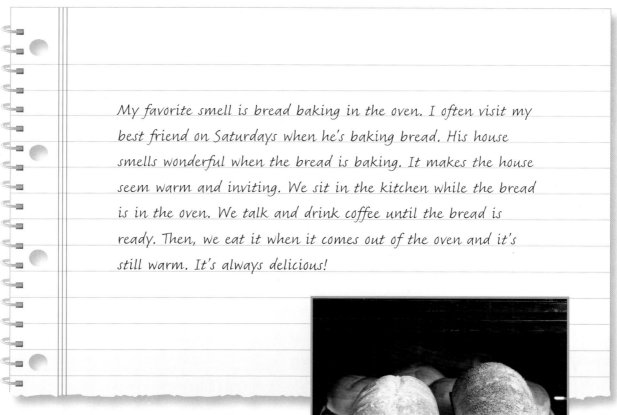

PREFERENCES

		You	Your Partner
1	What's your favorite taste?		
2	What's something you don't like the taste of?		
3	What's your favorite smell?		
4	What's a smell that you don't like?		
5	What's a sound that you don't like?		
6	What kind of music do you love to listen to?		
7	What kind of music don't you like to listen to?		
8	Describe something that you love to see.		

13 ▶ Writing

a Read the paragraph. What is the writer's favorite smell? How is it described?

My favorite smell is bread baking in the oven. I often visit my best friend on Saturdays when he's baking bread. His house smells wonderful when the bread is baking. It makes the house seem warm and inviting. We sit in the kitchen while the bread is in the oven. We talk and drink coffee until the bread is ready. Then, we eat it when it comes out of the oven and it's still warm. It's always delicious!

b Write a paragraph describing one of your answers from section 12. Describe it in as much detail as you can.

c Read other students' paragraphs. Which tastes, smells, sounds, and sights did students write about?

3 Big screen, small screen

✔ Movies and television
✔ Present perfect simple + *still / yet / already*; expressions of obligation and permission

1 ▶ Listening

a Look at the movie credits. What different jobs are there in making movies? What do you think the different jobs involve?

b **AUDIO** Listen to this interview with Jennifer. Which jobs has she done?
Which job would she like to do?

c **AUDIO** Listen again. Write T (true) or F (false).

F 1 Jennifer works in movies full-time.
___ 2 It was easy for her to finish writing her first screenplay.
___ 3 Making her movie took about four years.
___ 4 She wants to work with a famous actress in the future.
___ 5 She didn't enjoy shooting the movie because it was too tiring.
___ 6 She has many ideas for making future movies.

AUDIO Listen and check your answers. Discuss the false statements. Can you provide the correct information?

Director: JENNIFER B. KATZ

Producers: SARAH CAMERON, JENNIFER DANA, IKE McFADDEN

Editor: WYATT SMITH

Casting Director: ADRIENNE STERN

Actors: WENDY HOOPES, JAIME HARROLD, GLENN FITZGERALD, P.J. BROWN

d What job or part of movie-making do you think is most interesting?
What would you want to make a movie about?

2 ▶ Vocabulary: Types of movies

a Look at this list of movie types. Then read the movie listings page and circle five more types.

a drama   an action or adventure movie
a mystery or thriller   a love story

b Choose the four types of movies you like best. Compare answers with other students.

MOVIES

Bringing the Horses Home: Cowboys, horses, and the Wild West. An old-fashioned (western)!

All Over the Universe: Crazy adventures around the galaxy. Science fiction and comedy in one movie!

Bird World: A documentary about birds around the world.

Queen of the Mountain: Beautiful drawing and well-known actors' voices make this animated movie a "must see" for both kids and adults.

The Night: Ghosts, blood, and other scary things. Only for those who love a good horror movie!

3 ▶ Focus on Grammar

a Look at the chart. Answer the questions with *still*, *yet*, or *already*.

1 a Which adverb is used when something has happened sooner than expected?
  b Which two adverbs are used when something is expected to happen but (probably) has not happened?
2 Look at the position of each adverb. Which adverb can go in more than one place?

Present perfect simple + *still / yet / already*

I've **already** written and directed one movie.
I've written and directed one movie **already**.
He **still** hasn't quit his day job.
She hasn't done a lot of editing **yet**.
Have you done any editing **yet**?

Note: *Yet* is usually used in negative sentences and questions.
Still is used in negative sentences with the present perfect simple. It can be used in affirmative sentences and questions with other tenses. *He's still working. Are they still here?*

---

b Put the adverb in the correct place in each sentence.

Example   Have you watched that video ^yet^? (yet)

1 It's 5:00 p.m. and Joe hasn't finished the editing work. (still)
2 Sonia's been in three movies. (already)
3 I'm hungry. It's 11:00 a.m. and I haven't had breakfast. (still)
4 Let's go to a movie. I haven't seen the new one at the Lagoon Theater. (yet)

c Look at the picture and Conrad's To Do list. Say what Conrad has done or hasn't done. Use *still*, *yet*, or *already*.

Example   *He hasn't called Henry Lansing yet.* OR *He still hasn't called Henry Lansing.*

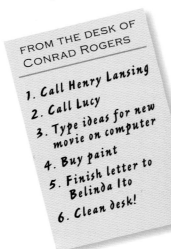

FROM THE DESK OF
CONRAD ROGERS

1. Call Henry Lansing
2. Call Lucy
3. Type ideas for new movie on computer
4. Buy paint
5. Finish letter to Belinda Ito
6. Clean desk!

d Talk about three things you have already done this week. Then talk about three things that you haven't done yet (or still haven't done), but that are on your To Do list.

Examples *I've already done my laundry.*
      I haven't finished a report for my boss yet.

4 Speaking

a Work in small groups. Ask and answer questions 1–6. Make notes of each person's answers.

b Exchange notes with another group. Look at that group's answers. Then, as a group, suggest one movie that each person in the other group might like.

1 What's your favorite movie? Why?
2 Who are your favorite actors/actresses or directors?
3 What types of movies don't you like? Why?
4 What movies have you seen more than once?
5 What's the best movie you've seen recently? What's the worst?
6 What new movie do you want to see, but haven't seen yet?

5 Language in Action: Opinions

a **AUDIO** Listen. Do Eddie and Maxine have the same opinion about the movie?

b **AUDIO** Try to complete the conversation with expressions from the chart below. Then listen and check your answers.

Eddie: That movie was really good!
Maxine: Hmm. ¹ *Do you think* so?
Eddie: What? Didn't you like it?
Maxine: Well, it was OK. But ² _____ it was a little unrealistic.
Eddie: ³ _____ it was…. OK, ⁴ _____ a little, but I think the acting was good.
Maxine: ⁵ _____. I just don't think they make thrillers like they used to. I always like the old-fashioned thrillers, you know, the classics.
Eddie: I like them, too. ⁶ _____, but I still don't think this movie was too bad.
Maxine: OK, let's agree to disagree on this one.

> **▼ Help Desk**
>
> *Let's agree to disagree* is a nice way to end a discussion when two people can't agree on something.

ASKING FOR OPINIONS	GIVING OPINIONS	AGREEING	DISAGREEING
What do you think?	I think / don't think…	I agree.	I disagree / don't agree.
Do you think…?	In my opinion…	Maybe…	I (still) don't think…
Don't you think…?	If you ask me…	I guess so.	I'm not sure.
		I suppose you're right.	

c Make your own conversations and give your opinions about the ideas below. Use expressions from the chart and give reasons. Try to either agree on something or "agree to disagree."

a type of movie   a movie you have both seen   a type of music (rock, classical, etc.)

Example   A: *I think action movies are great.*
                B: *I disagree. In my opinion, they're often violent…*

6 Writing: A movie review

a Read the review. What rating do you think the reviewer would give this movie? Why?

★★★★ = excellent   ★★★ = very good   ★★ = good   ★ = fair

REVIEWING THE CLASSICS:
Alfred Hitchcock's *Rear Window* (1954)

Rear Window is a genuine classic. It's a tense thriller that is still exciting to viewers today.

James Stewart plays the character of Jeff, a photographer who has broken his leg and has to stay in his apartment. Jeff starts watching his neighbors in order to pass the time. In one apartment, he notices some strange events which make him believe that one of his neighbors is a murderer. Grace Kelly, Stewart's co-star and possible love interest in the movie, helps him trap the killer.

One of the most interesting aspects of this movie is that the entire story takes place within Jeff's apartment or within view of it. This gives a fascinating and unusual viewpoint for all the events and characters in the story.

Even after all these years, this movie stands out as one of the best of its type. The acting is exceptional, and the directing is superb. Whether you watch it simply for the pleasure of a good thriller, or for the deeper suggestions about human nature, you won't be disappointed!

b Read the review again and answer the following questions.

  1 What type of movie is it?
  2 Who are the main characters? What happens in the movie?
  3 What is special about the movie?
  4 What are the summary points that end the review?

c Write a review of a movie you have seen. Use the questions in 6b as guidelines for your review.

d Have another student read your review and decide what rating you would give the movie.

7 *KnowHow*: Building vocabulary

a Look back at the review in 6a. Make a list of different words and expressions the reviewer uses to describe these aspects of the movie.

  1 The movie and movie type   *a genuine classic, a tense thriller, exciting*
  2 The actors / acting   _____
  3 The story   _____
  4 Other aspects   _____

b Work in pairs or groups. Can you add any more words of your own to the above lists?

c It's a good idea to try to use new words when you write. Look at the review you wrote in 6c again. Can you add some new words to make it even more descriptive?

8 ▶ Listening

a How much television do you watch? What types of shows do you like or not like?

b **AUDIO** Discuss questions 1 and 2 with a partner. Then listen to Charlie talking about his experience as an "extra" on a TV show and check your answers.

  1 What are "extras" in movies or on TV shows?
  2 Do extras usually have speaking parts on TV shows?

c **AUDIO** Listen again. Make notes on what Charlie says about these points.

  1 It's often not very exciting to be an extra because _____.
  2 It's interesting to be an extra when _____.
  3 He's been an extra in _____ shows.
  4 Typical things you do as an extra are _____.
  5 Charlie met the star of one show because _____.
  6 He'd like to be an extra in a _____.

d Do you know anyone who has been an extra for a movie or TV show? Which movie or TV show would you want to be an extra in? Why?

9 ▶ Vocabulary: Adjectives with -ed / -ing endings

a Look at the adjectives in bold in sentences 1 and 2. Which form of the adjective describes how the person feels? Which describes what makes him feel that way?

  1 The ending of the police drama was **confusing**. He didn't know who the criminal was.
  2 He was **confused** because he didn't understand the ending of the police drama.

b Fill in the blanks with an appropriate adjective. Choose the -ed or -ing form.

tired / tiring   surprised / surprising   frustrated / frustrating
relaxed / relaxing   fascinated / fascinating   interested / interesting
bored / boring   confused / confusing   disappointed / disappointing
excited / exciting

  1 Clare loves nature shows. She's _fascinated_ by nature.
  2 I'm too _____ to go out tonight. I'm going to watch TV.
  3 The soccer match was _____ because our team lost.
  4 This TV show is a little _____. Let's watch a different one.
  5 We were very _____ at the end of the movie. It was different from what we expected.
  6 The instructions for my VCR are _____. I can't understand them.

The puzzle is frustrating.
He's frustrated.

c Use the adjectives in 9b to talk about…

  1 the last time you were frustrated or fascinated by a movie.
  2 TV shows you think are exciting, boring, or interesting.

Examples *I was disappointed when I saw that movie. I didn't like it at all.*
         I watched a really exciting soccer game last week.

10 ▶ Focus on Grammar

a Look at the chart. Answer the questions below.

1 Which three expressions indicate obligation or necessity?
2 Which expression means to have (or not have) permission?
3 Which expression does not have a past form and is not followed by *to*?

Obligation and permission: Modals and expressions	
Present	*Past*
You **need to** be patient.	You **needed to** be patient.
You **have to** be patient.	You **had to** be patient.
You **must** be patient.	. . .
We **are / aren't allowed to** speak.	We **were / weren't allowed to** speak.

b Look at the notice below. There are five more mistakes. Find and correct them.

WORLDWIDE DRAMA

Information for extras:

- All actors have ^to^ arrive by 7 a.m.

- You must to be quiet on the set.
  Absolutely no talking!

- You not allowed to eat or drink on the set.

- You need check in. You are not
  allowed bring guests.

- Please come in costume. There is one dressing
  room if you need change.

- You must stay until the show is finished
  (or you won't get paid!).

c Work with a partner. Use the modals and expressions of obligation and permission to talk about...

1 things you were / weren't allowed to do as a child.
2 things you had to do as a child in school or at home.
3 things you must / have to / need to do at work or school now.

Example   *I wasn't allowed to stay up after 11:00 p.m. when I was a child.*

11 ▶ Reading

a Discuss the following questions in groups.

1 How do you think people typically feel when they watch TV? Do they feel relaxed, nervous, or energetic?
2 Do you think TV affects a person's intelligence? If so, how?

b Read the two articles quickly. What do the articles say about the questions in 11a?

A

In polls, two out of five adults and seven out of ten teenagers say they watch too much TV. Why do so many people worry about how much they watch?

A recent research study may give some clues about why TV has such a strong attraction for many people.

As you might expect, people watching TV reported feeling relaxed and passive. More surprising is that the sense of relaxation ended when the TV was turned off. But, the feeling of passivity continued. Participants commonly reported that TV took away their energy. They said they had more difficulty concentrating after watching TV than before.

In contrast, this was not reported after reading. And, after playing sports or doing hobbies, people report improvements in mood.

In the study, the longer people sat in front of the TV, the less satisfaction they said they got from it. Thus the irony of TV: people watch a great deal longer than they plan to, even though it is less rewarding to do so.

B

With all the criticism of a society of TV-watching "couch potatoes," it may be hard to believe that the human species is smarter than ever. But IQ* tests give evidence that people are getting smarter.

Research from the past twenty years shows that IQs around the world have gone up steadily. Researchers can't say exactly what is causing this change, but many think that watching TV and playing video games may be partly responsible.

There has been a "new kind of visual literacy" in the second half of the 20th century, says Ulric Neisser, a psychology professor who studies the

changes. "Movies and television and video games, with their images, have had an effect on the way people think…" he says. He believes that children do better on certain parts of IQ tests as a result.

Dr. Neisser's theory is in line with research findings. The most improvement has been in solving visual problems and answering questions creatively, not in areas such as facts, vocabulary, and arithmetic, which people learn in school.

* **IQ**= intelligence quotient

c Read the articles again. Are the statements true or false? Correct the false statements.

Article A:
1 Seven out of ten adults and two out of five teenagers feel that they watch too much TV.
2 In the study, people said they felt relaxed and passive while they watched TV.
3 People said they had more energy after they watched TV.
4 People said their mood was better after playing sports or doing hobbies.

Article B:
5 Research shows that IQs have gone up and down.
6 Dr. Neisser believes that TV, movies, and video games are affecting people's IQs.
7 Improvements have mainly been in the areas of vocabulary and facts, not in answering questions creatively.

d Find these words and expressions in the articles and match them to the definitions below.

a great deal   rewarding   alertness   mood   passive   steadily

Article A
1 _____: not active, with no reaction or interest
2 _____: a state of full attention
3 _____: the way a person feels at a particular time

Article B
4 _____: a lot of
5 _____: at a regular rate, constantly
6 _____: giving a feeling of satisfaction

e What do you think about the information in the articles? Does it change your group's answers in 11a in any way? If so, how?

12 ▶ Speaking

a Read the statements. Circle the number that indicates how much you agree or disagree.

	Strongly agree				Strongly disagree
1 Most people watch too much TV.	1	2	3	4	5
2 I watch too much TV.	1	2	3	4	5
3 TV can be very educational.	1	2	3	4	5
4 TV is bad for me.	1	2	3	4	5
5 There is too much violence in television and movies these days.	1	2	3	4	5
6 Children should be allowed to watch as much TV as they want.	1	2	3	4	5
7 TV and movies help us understand the world better.	1	2	3	4	5

b Compare your answers in pairs or groups. Give reasons for your opinions.

c Work in groups. See if you can make one summary statement about TV that you all agree on.

_TV_ _____

_____ .

Grammar

1 Read the text. What is Katie's job? What does she think about her job?

LIFE AS A CASTING DIRECTOR
Katie Waldren is a successful casting director. Her life sounds like a lot of fun, but is it a difficult job? "It really is," says Katie. "I work very long days. It takes a lot of concentration, and it's not easy to unwind. Even when I'm watching TV at home, I'm looking at the actors and taking notes. I only relax when I'm doing chores at home!"
Does she like her job? "I love it! I get frustrated sometimes, but it's very satisfying. I've finished one movie this year, a comedy, and now I'm working on a thriller. It's really exciting."

2 Complete the conversation.

Katie: Hey, have you seen Jane Layton's new TV show yet?
Walter: Yes, I have.
Katie: So ¹ _have I_ . It's terrible, isn't it?
Walter: You're right. I didn't enjoy it at all.
Katie: Neither ² _____ . But Manuel's new TV show is pretty good. I laughed a lot.
Walter: So ³ _____ . Are you planning to go to his party on Saturday?
Katie: No, I'm not.
Walter: Neither ⁴ _____ . I never enjoy his parties.

3 Complete Katie's e-mail to the director of the movie she's working on. Use the gerund or infinitive forms of the verbs in parentheses.

Carla,
I talked to David Bryanston today. He's very busy, but he wants ¹ _to do_ (do) the movie. He says he enjoys ² _____ (work) with you and he doesn't mind ³ _____ (lose) another job if he can work on this project. He would like ⁴ _____ (talk) to you face-to-face. He's planning ⁵ _____ (call) you tomorrow or Friday, and hopes ⁶ _____ (see) you sometime next week.
Talk to you later.
Katie

4 Fill in the blanks with the simple present or present continuous of the verbs in parentheses.

Dear Liz,

We ¹ _____ (work) hard these days on our next show. Ann, our costume designer, ² _____ (look) at the designs for Stella's dress in the party scene today. She says the designs ³ _____ (look) very good. Jake is responsible for the soundtrack. He ⁴ _____ (think) that it ⁵ _____ (not sound) exciting enough. Right now, he ⁶ _____ (think) about several solutions to this problem. There's a lot to do and it seems we ⁷ _____ (not have) enough time to do it all.

Sincerely,

Max

5 ▶ Walter is talking to his assistant. Complete the conversation. Use the present perfect simple.

Walter: Tim, [1] *have you called Mabel yet?*
(you / call / Mabel / yet)

Tim: No, I [2]_____
(not / call / her / yet), but I
[3]_____ (already / talk) to Jack Lewis and Darren Lee.

Walter: Good. I [4]_____
(still / not / hear from) Katie about that new project.

Tim: I [5]_____
(already / talk / to / her) about it. There's a note on your desk.

6 ▶ Complete the conversation about visiting an artist's home. Use *(not) allowed to* in present or past tenses.

Dan: We visited William Derwent's home last week.

Lily: The famous artist? How was it?

Dan: It was nice, but there are a lot of rules. For example, you
[1] *aren't allowed to* take any pictures at all, even in the garden, and you
[2]_____ wear shoes in the house.

Lily: Did you get to see his library?

Dan: Yes, we [3]_____ go inside, but we
[4]_____ touch anything.

7 ▶ Fill in the blanks with true information.

1 Yesterday, I had to _____.
2 Next week, I need to _____.
3 This afternoon, I must _____.
4 Sometime soon, I have to _____.

Vocabulary

8 ▶ Fill in the blanks with the correct words or expressions from the list.

celebration   fascinating   get better
sweep   chores   documentary

1 I have a lot of _____ to do today. I need to clean the house, go shopping, and wash the clothes.
2 We watched a _____ on TV last night about animals that live in the Arctic.

3 Were you bored during the movie?
— No, I thought it was _____.
4 Vanessa still doesn't feel well, but she is sure to _____ soon.
5 His family had a big _____ when he published his first book.
6 The floor is really dirty. Can you _____ it, please?

Recycling Center ♻

9 ▶ Write the comparative and superlative forms.

long	_____	longest
big	bigger	_____
good	_____	_____
hard	_____	_____
bad	_____	_____
difficult	more difficult	_____

10 ▶ Complete the paragraph with the correct comparative or superlative forms of the words in parentheses.

Chinese is one of the [1]_____ (hard) languages for English speakers to learn. The system of writing is much [2]_____ (complicated) than in English, but that isn't the [3]_____ (bad) problem. What makes it [4]_____ (hard) than other languages is its treatment of time, which seems [5]_____ (simple) than in English but is actually [6]_____ (difficult) for English speakers to understand.

Fun Spot

How many words can you make using letters from the word SYNESTHESIA? When you have finished, score yourself.
10–15 words = Great!
6–9 words = Good!
3–5 words = OK.
1–3 words = We know you can do better!

Examples: *these, is*

4 In the mind's eye

✔ Memories and memory techniques
✔ Past continuous; comparatives

1 ▶ Listening

a Look at the photos. What's happening in each one?

b **AUDIO** Listen. Put the photos in the order Kristy and Hugh talk about them. __ __ __

c **AUDIO** Listen again. Write T (true) or F (false).

1 Hugh remembers everything about the party. __
2 Hugh came back later than expected for the party. __
3 Kenny helped him move into his apartment. __
4 It was easy to get everything into the apartment. __
5 Kristy got hurt on the first day of the trip. __
6 She broke her arm. __

d Do you like looking at photos from different times in your life? Why?

2 ▶ Vocabulary: Common expressions with *come* and *go*

a Read the sentences. Match the expressions in bold (1–7) with their meanings (a–h).

1 You **went out** and you **came back** early.   *1c* __   a continue
2 We shouted, "Surprise!" when you **came in**.   __   b happening
3 Everyone **came over** and helped me move.   __   c left for a short time
4 Weren't you there?   __   d left for a longer time (for
—No, I **went away** that weekend.   example, a few days)
5 **Come on**! We're going to be late for the movie. __   e entered
6 **Go on**, don't stop. Tell me the whole story.   __   f hurry
7 What was **going on** in this picture?   __   g visited
                                            h returned

b Fill in the blanks with the correct form of an expression with *come* or *go*.

1 "*Come on*! I don't want to miss the bus," Louis said.
2 I knocked at the door. "_____!" said a voice.
3 My neighbors aren't home. They _____ last week.
4 Do you want to _____ to my house tomorrow?
5 I have to leave my office now, but I'll _____ at 5:00.
6 Did you _____ last night? You didn't answer the phone.

▼ Help Desk

The use of *come* and *go* depends on the position of the speaker.
Come usually indicates movement toward the speaker.
Go usually indicates movement away from the speaker.

*I **went over** to Kristy's house.*

*Kristy **came over** to my house.*

3 ▶ Focus on Grammar

a Look at the chart. Answer the questions about the verb forms.

1 Which form describes actions in progress in the past? (simple past / past continuous)
2 Which form is used for a shorter, completed action in the past (often interrupting an action in progress)? (simple past / past continuous)
3 How do you form the past continuous?

Past continuous	
Background to a story	It was a beautiful day. The sun **was shining**, and we **were getting** ready for our ski trip. Everyone **was having** a lot of fun.
Interrupted action	I **was standing** at the top of the hill when someone r**an** into me. You **came** in the door while we **were putting up** decorations for the party.

b Fill in the blanks with the past continuous or simple past.

1 They _were leaving_ (leave) the office when the phone ___rang___ (ring).
2 It _____ (start) to rain while the children _____ (play) outside.
3 Marcia _____ (wait) when Henry _____ (arrive) at the restaurant.
4 Josh's car _____ (break) down while he _____ (drive) home yesterday.
5 When we _____ (come) into the office, they _____ (talk) about politics.
6 I _____ (see) an old friend while I _____ (walk) to work this morning.

c Circle the correct verb forms in the paragraph.

I had two accidents last month. First, my friend and I ¹(rode / were riding) our bicycles and it ²(rained / was raining). We ³(rode / were riding) fast because we ⁴(wanted / were wanting) to get home. I ⁵(turned / was turning) the corner when suddenly, a cat ⁶(ran / was running) in front of my bike. I tried to stop, but I ⁷(fell / was falling) and ⁸(broke / was breaking) my arm. Then, a few days after that, I ⁹(walked / was walking) up the stairs in my apartment when I ¹⁰(hurt / was hurting) my ankle. Fortunately, I ¹¹(didn't break / wasn't breaking) it, but it wasn't a good month!

d Think of something unusual or surprising that happened to you. Describe what happened using the past continuous and simple past.

Example   *I was driving my car the other day. It was a beautiful day. I was listening to the radio when suddenly, my car made a strange noise…*

4 ▶ Speaking

a What's your earliest memory? Try to remember as much detail as possible. Use these questions to help.

How old were you?   Where were you?
What were you doing?   What happened?

b Work in small groups. Take turns describing your memories. Then discuss the questions.

1 Whose memory is the earliest?
2 Who remembers the most details?
3 How accurate do you think these kinds of memories are?

5 ▶ Reading

a Look at the photograph and painting of the same village in Italy. Describe the pictures. What similarities and differences can you find?

b Read the article. What's surprising about Magnani's way of painting?

A Memory ARTIST

The place in these pictures is a town in Italy called Pontito. Franco Magnani is an artist who has painted over one hundred pictures of Pontito, his childhood home. The paintings are surprisingly accurate. This is even more suprising because Magnani does not live there now and has not returned to the town since he left in 1958. Until recently, he had not even seen a photograph of the town. He paints his pictures entirely from memory.

Magnani is a self-taught artist. He began painting in 1965, eight years after he left Pontito, because he was sick and unable to work. His first painting was of the house where he was born. After that, painting scenes of his native village became the focus of his life. Magnani says that he drew or painted particular scenes to bring back pleasant memories.

For example, a picture of the hills around the village reminds him of the joy he felt walking through the hills with his father as a child.

Many of his paintings begin with a kind of memory flash, where a certain scene suddenly comes into his head. He feels urgency to get the scene onto paper immediately. The "flash" he describes is not static like a photograph. When he closes his eyes to picture a part of the town, he can look around and "see" in several directions. In fact, he moves his body, turning left and right to imagine what would be on the left or on the right in a scene of Pontito.

Most of the paintings seem more inviting than the scenes in the photographs. Through the paintings, Magnani creates a world as quiet and dreamy as a childhood memory.

c Read the article in 5b again. Write T (true), F (false), or NI (no information).

1 Magnani left his hometown in 1958. ___
2 He uses photographs of the village when he paints. ___
3 He always wanted to be an artist. ___
4 When he began painting, he didn't have a job. ___
5 Some of his paintings are related to good childhood memories. ___
6 He thinks about a scene for a long time before he starts to draw or paint it. ___
7 The scenes he sees in his mind are exactly like photographs. ___
8 He would like to go back and visit Pontito again. ___

d Complete the sentences with a word from the article. (1) = paragraph number.

1 A painting where all the details are exactly correct is very _accurate_. (1)
2 When you don't have a teacher and learn something by yourself, you are _____. (2)
3 The place where you were born is your _____ town or city. (2)
4 A feeling of great happiness is _____. (2)
5 Something that doesn't move or change is _____. (3)
6 Something that is attractive and pleasant is _____. (4)

e Why do you think Magnani remembers Pontito so well? How well do you remember places?

6 Writing

a Think of a place from your past. Imagine it in as much detail as possible. Then write a paragraph describing what it was like.

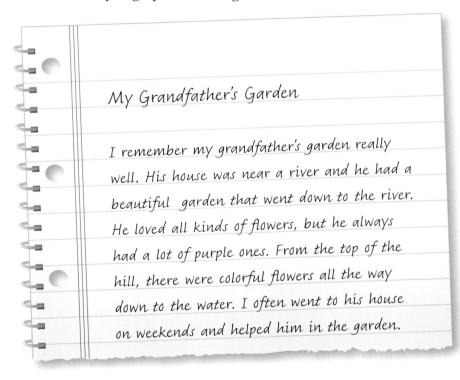

My Grandfather's Garden

I remember my grandfather's garden really well. His house was near a river and he had a beautiful garden that went down to the river. He loved all kinds of flowers, but he always had a lot of purple ones. From the top of the hill, there were colorful flowers all the way down to the water. I often went to his house on weekends and helped him in the garden.

b Work with a partner. Take turns reading your descriptions. Ask your partner questions for more detail about what he or she has written.

7 ▶ Focus on Grammar

a Look at the pictures and the sentences in the chart. Answer questions 1–3 below.

1 Do you use *-er* with short adjectives (one syllable) or with long adjectives (two or more syllables)? When do you use *more* and *less*?

2 How do you say that two things are equal?

3 Does *not as … as* mean "less" or "more"?

$125

$125

Comparatives: Review and extension

adjective + -er + *than*	The photograph is small**er than** the painting.
more / less + *adjective* + than	The photograph is **more colorful than** the painting. The painting is **less colorful than** the photograph.
as + *adjective* + **as**	The photograph is **as expensive as** the painting.
not + **as** + *adjective* + **as**	The photograph is **not as big as** the painting.

b Write other sentences with the same meaning. Use the forms in parentheses.

1 The painting is bigger than the photograph. (not as…as)
 The photograph is not as big as the painting.

2 The outdoor scene is more beautiful than the painting of the house. (less)
 _____

3 The painting and the photograph are both pretty. (as…as)_____

4 The photograph is less interesting than the painting. (not as…as)
 _____

5 These photographs aren't as expensive as the paintings. (more) _____

c Make sentences comparing the photos. Use *-er*, *more* or *less*, *as…as*, and *not as…as*.

8 ▶ Listening

a **AUDIO** Match the memory words (1–5) with the correct definitions (a–e). Listen and check.

1 remember   _1d_   a   not remember something; lose the memory of something
2 forget   __   b   help someone remember something
3 remind   __   c   forgetting things frequently
4 memorize   __   d   bring something back into your mind
5 absent-minded __   e   learn something so that you can remember it exactly

b Are you absent-minded? What do you do to help yourself remember things?

c **AUDIO** Listen. What are two reasons Tatiana's memory is special or unusual?

d **AUDIO** Listen again and circle the correct answer.

Tatiana Cooley

1 Tatiana can remember (60 of 100 / 70 of 100 / 75 of 100) names and faces after 15 minutes.
2 She has (five or six / six or seven / seven or eight) brothers and sisters.
3 She feels that remembering everyday things and memorizing things are (the same process / similar processes / different processes).
4 She believes (anyone / no one else / some people) can train themselves to memorize.
5 She uses (many different / three / two) techniques to memorize.
6 She realized she was good at memorizing (as a child / in college / in her first job).

e Which kind of memory do you think is more useful or important: memorizing or remembering everyday things? Give reasons for your answer.

9 ▶ Vocabulary: Compound adjectives

a Underline the compound adjectives in this paragraph.

My cousin, Oliver, is a <u>well-known</u> musician. He's very good, but he's also very absent-minded. He always keeps a To Do list to remember things. He has a full-time job and travels a lot. He just bought a brand-new house, but he isn't there much because he's always traveling. He's a well-dressed man; he loves nice clothes. He's left-handed, and he says that's why he's so creative. I don't agree because I'm right-handed, and I'm very creative, too!

b Fill in the blanks with the adjectives below.

right-handed   good-looking   short-sleeved   full-time

1 We always wear _short-sleeved_ shirts in summer.
2 He's very _____. He looks like a movie star.
3 I broke my right arm. It's difficult to do things because I'm _____.
4 Monique just got a _____ job. She only worked ten hours a week before.

c Write five sentences about yourself or people and things you know. Use as many compound adjectives as you can.

Example   *I work in an office. I had a part-time job before, but now I have a full-time job.*

10 ▶ Language in Action: Trying to remember

a **AUDIO** Listen. What are they trying to remember? Do they remember it?

b **AUDIO** Listen again. Check the expressions you hear in the conversation.

> **MEMORY EXPRESSIONS**
> ___ I can't remember.
> ___ I can't think of it.
> ___ Let me think.
> ___ It's on the tip of my tongue.
> ___ It'll come to me in a minute.
> ___ I'll think of it in a minute.
> ___ Remind me to…

c Work with a partner. Use expressions from 10b and make your own conversations about trying to remember. Use these ideas (or your own).

the name of a restaurant   a person's name   a song title   the name of a movie

Example   A: *Do you remember the name of that restaurant on Hill Street?*
              B: *Which one?*
              A: *The Korean one next to the library…*

11 ▶ *KnowHow*: Sentence stress (unstressed words)

a **AUDIO** A sentence has both stressed and unstressed words or syllables. Look at the sentence and listen. Which words are unstressed?

　　•　　　•　　　　•　　•
It's on the tip of my tongue.

b Mark the stressed words and syllables in these sentences and then practice saying the sentences. Remember not to stress the unstressed words.

1   It'll come to me in a second.
2   I'll think of it in a minute.
3   This one's better than that one.

c **AUDIO** Listen and check your sentence stress.

> ▼ **Help Desk**
>
> It is easier to understand English if you know that some words are stressed and some are unstressed in a sentence.
>
> Is sentence stress different in your language?

Reading and Speaking

a Read the articles about "Memory Techniques" and follow the instructions.

Taking a Trip

Read the shopping list once. Then cover it and try to write down the list in exactly the same order.

soap	orange juice
shampoo	salad dressing
newspaper	ice cream
cookies	milk

Now, try using the trip technique and see if it's easier to remember. Imagine a short trip that you know well (for example, your trip to work). Think of familiar landmarks on this trip. Then associate each item on the list with a landmark on your trip.

You can use this technique to remember any kind of list. Use a long trip if you have a long list.

For example:

1. soap and shampoo: a large bar of soap and bottle of shampoo in front of my apartment door.

2. newspaper: piles of newspapers at the top of the stairway in my building.

3. cookies: piles of cookies by the car.

A is for apple

Answer the questions below. Time yourself for each set.

1 Name a fruit beginning with the letter *L*
2 Name an animal beginning with the letter *C*
3 Name a country beginning with the letter *F*
4 Name a vegetable beginning with the letter *P*

Set one: Time

1 Name a fruit ending with the letter *H*
2 Name an animal ending with the letter *T*
3 Name a country ending with the letter *Y*
4 Name a vegetable ending with the letter *T*

Set two: Time

Most people complete set one faster than set two. This suggests that using the first letter of a word is a common way to organize words in our memories, but that using the last letter is not common.

b How much of the information in the articles is new or surprising to you?

c How easy are these things for you to remember? Circle a number (1 = easy, 3 = more difficult).

1	People's names	1	2	3
2	Birthdays and other important dates	1	2	3
3	Phone numbers and addresses	1	2	3
4	New vocabulary and irregular verbs	1	2	3
5	Information for a test or exam	1	2	3
6	Family history and memories	1	2	3
7	Errands and things to buy at the store	1	2	3

Now compare answers in small groups. Discuss the best techniques for remembering things in each situation.

5 Stuff of life

✔ Favorite objects and how things work
✔ Relative clauses (subject); phrasal verbs

1 ▶ Reading

a Describe the picture. Do you know who this person is? What do you notice about his guitar?

b Read the article quickly. Choose the best summary.

1 Nelson uses a lot of different guitars, but he has one that he likes best.
2 Nelson's guitar is old and worn, so he wants to repair it or buy a new one.
3 Nelson always uses the same guitar. It's old and worn, but he likes it.

c Read the article again. Answer the questions.

1 When did Nelson get his guitar?
2 What are two ways the guitar is unusual?
3 Why doesn't Nelson want to fix the hole?
4 How did he get the guitar?

d What do you think about age and quality? Do you think old things are better? Do you think some things today are made differently than in the past? Consider these items.

> **buildings   cars   clothes**
> **household appliances**
> **furniture   art**

A Special Guitar

Willie Nelson is a well-known country singer. His guitar, nicknamed "Trigger," is almost as famous as he is. Nelson has had the guitar for more than 30 years and doesn't play any other guitar.

Much like Nelson, the guitar has come a long way. It is worn and weathered now. He's played it so much that it has a large hole in the front. Nelson is so sentimental about the hole that he won't get it repaired.

Another reason Nelson loves his guitar is that many of his friends have autographed it. Nelson estimates that the guitar has about 100 signatures from friends, musicians, and other associates, all scratched on the surface with a knife. Nelson bought the guitar in 1969 without seeing it. He had a different guitar before that, but that one got broken. He sent the broken one to a friend for repair, but his friend said he couldn't fix it. Nelson asked what other guitars he had. His friend said he had a classical guitar that cost $750, and Nelson bought it.

"And that's how I got it, " says Nelson. "Right off the shelf, unseen from a thousand miles away. When I got it, I knew that I had picked up something special. I like to just sit around a room and play it. I like to write on it. I just like the sound of it. "

2 ▶ Focus on Grammar

a Relative clauses give more information about a person or thing. Look at the chart. Then match the words *who*, *which*, and *that* with the correct use (A–C).

1 who __   2 which __   3 that __

A = used for people and things   B = used only for people   C = used only for things

Relative clauses (subject)	
Who is Willie Nelson? He's a musician **who** plays country music. **that** plays country music.	Which guitar is his? It's the guitar **that** has a hole in it. **which** has a hole in it.

Note: When referring to things, *that* is more common than *which* as the subject of a relative clause.

b Use *who* or *that* and write one sentence.

1 Nicole Shelby is a musician. She plays jazz music.
   Nicole Shelby is a musician who plays jazz music .
2 She has made two CDs. The CDs have won awards.
   _____
3 She often plays in a club. The club has live music every
   night. _____
4 Nicole and her husband live in a house. The house has two pianos in it. _____
5 They have a son. Their son is two years old. _____

> ▼ **Help Desk**
>
> Don't forget the relative pronoun with this type of relative clause.
>
> *He's a musician who plays country music.* (Not: ~~He's a musician plays country music.~~)

c Think of an example for each category (1–4) but don't say what it is. Write a definition. See if another student can guess what it is.

Example (1) *This is a person who cooks food in a restaurant.* (a chef)

1 a job / occupation   2 an animal   3 a fruit   4 a vegetable

3 ▶ Vocabulary: Adjectives for materials

a AUDIO Fill in the blanks. Then listen and check your answers.

glass   wooden   metal

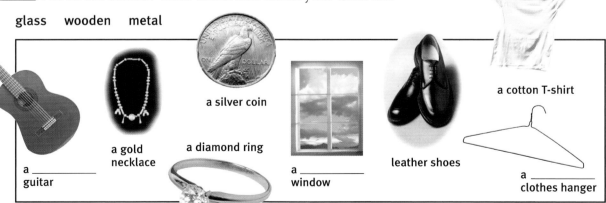

a silver coin

a gold necklace

a diamond ring

a cotton T-shirt

leather shoes

a _____ guitar

a _____ window

a _____ clothes hanger

b Think of five everyday things. Use materials from 3a to describe them. Compare answers.

Examples *a wooden table, a cotton sweater, a gold ring*

36

4 Listening

a Look at the pictures. Describe each of the items. Which item(s) do you think is (are) important to each person?

Mauricio   Elaine   Lars and Ruth   Bruce   Mia

b **AUDIO** Listen and check your guesses.

c **AUDIO** Listen again. Write one thing you hear about each item. Then compare your answers with a partner.

1 ring _____   4 stereo and CDs _____
2 motorcycle and backpack _____   5 watch _____
3 basket of family memories _____

5 Speaking

a Work in small groups. Take turns talking about an object that is important to you. Make a chart for your group.

Student name	What is it?	Why is it important?
1		
2		

b Discuss your answers as a class. Decide:

Which item is the oldest?   Which is the most practical?   Which is the most unusual?

Language in Action: What's it called?

a **AUDIO** Listen. What is Lily trying to fix?

Ken: What's the matter?
Lily: I'm fixing this picture frame, but I need something to turn this little thing.
Ken: Do you want a screwdriver?
Lily: No, ¹_____ a screwdriver, but it's smaller. ²_____ turn really small screws.
³_____
Ken: Is this it? ⁴_____ a really small screwdriver.
Lily: Yes, that's it. Thanks.
Ken: You know, I think this is just another kind of screwdriver.
Lily: Oh really? Well, whatever it is, I fixed the picture frame with it!

b **AUDIO** Try to complete the conversation with expressions from the chart. Then listen and check.

ASKING THE NAME OF SOMETHING	SAYING YOU DON'T KNOW THE NAME OF SOMETHING	DESCRIBING IT
What do you call the thing that…? Do you know the name of this thing?	I'm not sure what it's called. I don't know the name of it.	It's (big, small, blue). It looks like…. OR It's like…but…. You use it to…. OR You use it for….

c Work with a partner. Use expressions from the chart and make conversations about these things.

Answer key: 1. can opener 2. scissors 3. paring knife 4. hammer

> ▼ **Help Desk**
>
> **You use it + infinitive**
> *You use it to put a picture on the wall.*
>
> **You use it for + verb -ing**
> *You use it for putting a picture on the wall.*

 KnowHow: **When you don't know a word**

a What do you do if you don't know a word? Look at these strategies. Which ones have you used?

At the moment:	Later:
• Describe what it looks like or what it's for. • Use mime or gesture. • Use a word that is close in meaning. • Use a substitute word. (In English, people often use *thingy* or *thingamajig*.)	• Look it up in a dictionary. • Make a note of the word for the future.

b Think of something you don't know the name of in English. Work with a partner. Practice at least three of the above strategies.

8 ▶ Listening

a Look at these objects. Discuss questions 1 and 2 below.

A remote control for a TV A DVD player A hair dryer A coffee maker A toaster oven A microwave oven

1 Which things do you use most often? Which do you use least often?
2 Which of the items do you think are most difficult to operate? Which are the easiest?

b 【AUDIO】 Listen to the conversation. Which object are they talking about? What's the problem?

c 【AUDIO】 Listen again. Which of these things do they do? Which don't they do? Write Y (Yes) or N (No).

1 turn the temperature dial	__	5 have a cup of coffee	__
2 turn on the toaster oven	__	6 turn down the temperature	__
3 press the "toast" button	__	7 turn off the oven	__
4 turn up the temperature	__	8 throw the sandwich away	__

9 ▶ Vocabulary: Parts of things and how things work

a Look at the diagram and instructions. Put words from the diagram into the blanks in the instructions.

b Work with a partner. Look at the photos in 8a again. Name as many parts of the objects as you can and say how they work.

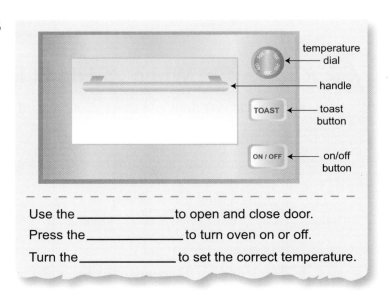

temperature dial
handle
TOAST — toast button
ON / OFF — on/off button

Use the _____ to open and close door.

Press the _____ to turn oven on or off.

Turn the _____ to set the correct temperature.

10 ▶ Focus on Grammar

a Phrasal verbs are made up of more than one word (for example, *turn on, take out...*). Look at the chart. Which type of word <u>cannot</u> go after the second word in the phrasal verb?

> **Structures with phrasal verbs: Word order**
>
> How do you **turn on** <u>the oven</u>?   Can you **take out** <u>the sandwiches</u>?
> How do you **turn** <u>the oven</u> **on**?   Can you **take** <u>the sandwiches</u> **out**?
> How do you **turn** <u>it</u> **on?**   Can you **take** <u>them</u> **out**?
> Not: ~~How do you **turn on** it~~?   Not: ~~Can you **take out** them~~?
>
> **Note:** Not all phrasal verbs are separable. *Get on the bus.* (Not: ~~Get the bus on.~~)

b Find four more phrasal verbs in section 8c and fill in the blanks.

1 *put on* = place something (clothes, shoes, jewelry, eyeglasses, etc.) on your body
2 *take off* = remove something (especially clothes)
3 *put away* = put something into the place where it is kept
4 *pick up* = lift something up
5 *put down* = place something on a surface (for example, the floor or a table)
6 _____ = increase the sound or heat that something produces
7 _____ = reduce the sound or heat that something produces
8 _____ = stop a machine from working
9 _____ = put something in a garbage can

c Fill in the blanks with phrasal verbs and the words in parentheses.

1 Can you please __*turn up the TV*__ / __*turn the TV up*__? I can't hear it. (the TV)
2 Don't forget to _____ when you're finished. Don't leave it on. (the oven)
3 Where are my keys? I thought I _____ right here. (them)
4 I'll _____. It's getting dark in here. (the lights)
5 Oh no, the milk tastes bad. Someone forgot to _____. (it)
6 Why are these papers on the floor? Let's _____. (them)

d Answer the questions with complete sentences.

1 What is the first thing you turned on this morning?
2 What do you always turn off when you leave your house or apartment?
3 What's one thing you sometimes forget to put away?
4 What's the last thing you threw away?

11 ▶ Speaking

a Complete the statements with your own words. Then compare answers with a partner.

1 One household object that I can't live without is _____ because _____.
2 An invention or gadget that is <u>not</u> useful for me is _____ because _____.
3 The most important invention in the last hundred years was _____ because _____.
4 Someone should invent something to _____.

b Work in groups or as a class and discuss your answers. Then, as a group, try to agree on the most and least useful inventions of the last hundred years.

12 ▶ Reading

a Read the article quickly. Why are Kenji Kawakami's inventions special? How many are there?

Inventing Creatively

Do you dislike dusting? What about some slippers for your cat to wear? The cat slippers pick up dust as the cat moves around your house. Of course, it works better if you don't have a lazy cat.

You have an itch on your back. You can't reach it, but a friend can help you if he or she knows exactly where the itch is. How about a T-shirt with a grid to help locate the itch?

These are interesting ideas, but obviously not really practical for one or more reasons. This is the essence and contradiction of *Chindogu*, an invented term which combines two Japanese words to mean "unusual tool." Typically, Chindogu solves an everyday problem, but creates new problems in the process.

Chindogu was created by Kenji Kawakami, an inventor who thought of these ideas because he was frustrated with society's materialism. He created Chindogu not for financial reasons but to improve his creativity. Kawakami's inventions will not appear in a store near you, but his ideas have become popular around the world. Chindogu has now evolved into a kind of philosophy with ten major principles, including the rule that the inventions cannot be for real use or for sale. Also, while Chindogu are often funny, humor cannot be the sole reason for creating them.

Kawakami, who has two books of the inventions, believes that Chindogu can encourage new ideas and thinking. Some corporations have bought his books to help their employees do this, too.

There are at least 500 different Chindogu already and people around the world have started contributing their own ideas for Chindogu.

So, if there's an everyday problem that bothers you, maybe it's time to be creative and think up your own Chindogu!

b Read the article again. Complete the sentences.

1 Two examples of Chindogu are _____.
2 The contradiction of Chindogu is that _____.
3 Kenji Kawakami started these inventions because _____.
4 One example of a Chindogu principle is _____.
5 Some corporations use Kawakami's books to _____ among employees.

c Find words 1–6 in the article. Circle the definition (a or b). (1) = paragraph number.

1 slippers (1)   (a) soft shoes you wear indoors   b shoes you wear outdoors
2 itch (2)   a something that hurts   b a feeling on your skin that you want to scratch

3 grid (2)   a a painting   b a simple diagram with lines
4 evolved (4)   a changed or developed   b stayed the same
5 sole (5)   a many   b only
6 bothers (8)   a disturbs or irritates   b helps

d What do you think about the idea of Chindogu?

13 Writing and Speaking

a Match this description to the correct picture.

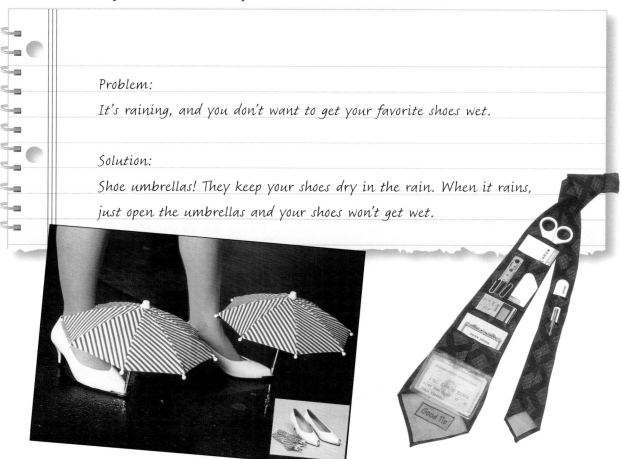

Problem:

It's raining, and you don't want to get your favorite shoes wet.

Solution:

Shoe umbrellas! They keep your shoes dry in the rain. When it rains, just open the umbrellas and your shoes won't get wet.

b Work with a partner. Think of an everyday problem related to one of the following areas (or use your own ideas) and think of a Chindogu for it. Remember that it should not be practical!

> sleeping or waking up   commuting or driving   rainy weather   eating and drinking   keeping clean

c Write a description of your Chindogu.

d Work in groups or as a class. Compare and discuss your Chindogu ideas.

6 *Interesting characters*

✔ Friends and other interesting people
✔ Present perfect + *for / since*; simple past + *ago*;
gerunds as subjects and after prepositions

1 ▶ Reading

a Look at the list of types of friends. What do you think each type is like?

> **Best Friend**
> **Special-Interest Friend**
> **New Friend**
> **Ex-Friend**
> **Train or Bus Friend**
> **Wild Friend**

b Read the article. Fill in the blanks with the types of friends from above.

c Do any of your friends fit into these categories? Do you have different types of friends?

2 ▶ Speaking

a Work with a partner. Choose one of the types of friends below (or use your own idea). Discuss how to describe the type and make some notes.

> **Work Friend**
> **Old Friend**
> **E-mail Friend**
> **Sports Friend**
> **Class Friend**

b Work in groups. Describe the type you chose in 2a.

Types *of* Friends

❶ New Friend

Generally speaking, a person who can do no wrong until you've had more time together. This friend is more likely to enjoy your stories, agree with your opinions, and show up on time. It's also easier to be who you are with this kind of friend, as opposed to who you *were*, which is what usually happens with old friends.

❷ _____

You chat with this person on your way to and from work. This is a person who, like you, is apparently *always* interested in the weather and what's happening with the local sports team.

❸ _____

You're no longer friends— it's usually better not to ask about it!

❹ _____

You're always surprised at this person's unusual behavior. Sometimes it's good and sometimes it's crazy, but you are always entertained. Boring people usually need a friend like this!

❺ _____

Who knows where and how you meet, but there's something special about this friendship. This is the friend you can depend on for everything. This friend listens to you, helps you out, and is always there for you.

❻ _____

A lot of friendships form around a shared interest, for example, playing soccer, cooking, or sky-diving. It's usually a good way to make friends because you're interested in the same thing.

3 ▶ Vocabulary: Prepositions with verbs and adjectives

a Complete the expressions below with the correct prepositions. (The expressions are in the article on page 43.)

Verbs	Adjectives
think *about*	similar *to*
worry *about*	good *at*
look *at*	interested _____
agree _____	surprised _____
depend _____	
listen _____	
ask _____	

b Fill in the blanks with the correct prepositions.

1 Tim and Lucia are both interested _in_____ computers. That's how they met.
2 Margie and I aren't friends anymore. I could never depend _____ her.
3 Please listen _____ John. It's important.
4 Alex doesn't always agree _____ me, but he's still my best friend.
5 Ask Michiko _____ the party. I don't know anything about it.
6 I was surprised _____ their behavior. They usually act differently.

4 ▶ Listening

a **AUDIO** Listen to Russell and Audrey talk about their friends. What is the main difference between their ideas about friends?

b **AUDIO** Listen again. Who might say each of these statements? Write *Russell*, *Audrey*, or *both*. Then give reasons for your answers.

1 I moved to this city because of work.
   Russell. He didn't live here before he got
   this job.

2 I don't see my best friend often.
   _____

3 I've known my best friend for a long
   time. _____

4 I do a lot of sports activities with people
   from the office. _____

5 I know a lot of musicians.
   _____

6 It makes sense to have a lot of friends
   from work. _____

c Which person's idea about friends is most similar to yours? Explain your answer.

5 ▶ Focus on Grammar

a Look at the chart and answer the questions.

1 Which tense is used for a completed action in the past?
2 Which tense is used for something that began in the past and continues now?
3 When do you use *ago*? When do you use *for* and *since*?

Present perfect simple	Simple past
I've **lived** here **for** two years.	I **moved** here two years **ago.**
Audrey **has been** in the band **since** last year.	She **started** playing in the band a year **ago.**

Note: Use *for* with a period of time: *ten days, a month, five years.*
Use *since* with the starting point: *1998, last week, Friday.*

b Make sentences with the present perfect simple and *for* or *since* or with the simple past.

1 I / know / my best friend / a long time.   *I've known my best friend for a long time.*
2 Ernesto / get / that job / three years ago.   _____
3 Melissa / start / an Italian class / last week.   _____
4 They / know / Pete and Irene / ten years.   _____
5 Our parents / live / in the same house / 1979.   _____
6 Yuko and Alicia / work / together / June.   _____

c Ask and answer questions with the simple past or present perfect simple and the ideas below.

   live   move   know   meet   apartment / house   town / city   friends / relatives

Example   *How long have you lived in your house?* OR *When did you move to your house?*

6 ▶ Language in Action: Meeting and introducing people

a **AUDIO** Listen. Which person has seen Annie in the library?

b **AUDIO** Listen again. Check the expressions you hear in the conversation.

INTRODUCING PEOPLE	RECOGNIZING SOMEONE
___ I'd like you to meet…	___ I think we've met before.
___ This is (name).	___ Have we met before?
___ Do you know (name)?	___ You look familiar.
___ Have you met (name)?	___ I think I recognize you.
___ It's nice to meet you.	___ That's why I recognize you.

▼ Help Desk

When you introduce people, it's nice to give a little information about each person.

Annie, this is Philip. We work in the same office. Philip, Annie is a friend from my hiking club.

c Work in groups. Use expressions from the chart and take turns introducing people.

Example   **Tom:** *Lea, I'd like you to meet my friend Hugo. We work together.*
              Lea: *It's nice to meet you, Hugo.*

KnowHow: Pronunciation of the schwa /ə/

a AUDIO Listen. The underlined syllable(s) in the words below all have vowels with a schwa sound. Can all vowels be pronounced with the schwa sound?

1 introduce   Please int<u>ro</u>duce us.
2 famili<u>ar</u>   You look famili<u>ar</u>.
3 togeth<u>er</u>   Let's get togeth<u>er</u> soon.
4 prom<u>i</u>se   I prom<u>i</u>se I'll be there.
5 s<u>u</u>ccess   The business was a s<u>u</u>ccess.

> ▼ **Help Desk**
>
> The schwa is an unstressed vowel sound. It is the most common vowel sound in English.

b AUDIO Underline the schwa in these words. Listen and check. Then practice saying the words and sentences in 7a and b.

  advice   cousin   machine   tonight   recognize   problem   similar   adventure

 Listening: Song

a AUDIO Read the song. Try to fill in the blanks with the lyrics below. Then listen to the song and check your answers.

  a   To make that day last long
  b   I had some friends but they're gone
  c   Waiting for my new friends to come
  d   There is no one here beside me
  e   Something came and took them away

b AUDIO Listen again and answer the questions.

  1   How important are friends to the singer? What lines in the song tell you that?
  2   Does the singer have a lot of friends right now? What does she hope for the future?

c What other songs do you know on the topic of friends?

Friends
Bette Midler

And I am all alone
¹ *There is no one here beside me*
And my problems have all gone
There is no one to deride me

But you got to have friends
The feeling's oh so strong
You got to have friends
2 _____

3 _____
4 _____

And from the dusk 'til the dawn
Here is where I'll stay

Standing at the end of the road, boys
5 _____

I don't care if I'm hungry or poor
I'm gonna get me some of them

Cause you got to have friends
Da, da, da, da…. friends
That's right, oh yeah, yeah, yeah
I said you gotta have some friends
I'm talking about friends, that's right, friends
Friends, friends, friends…

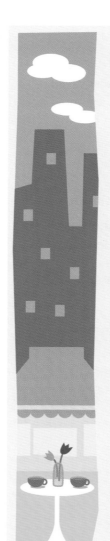

9 ▶ Listening

a Look at the pictures of some personality tests. Do you know anything about them? Can you think of other personality tests?

b AUDIO Listen to the interview. Which kind of test from the picture is <u>not</u> discussed?

c AUDIO Listen again. Answer the questions.

1 What is one reason people might use personality tests?
2 What is *graphology*?
3 Why is it hard to know how accurate personality tests are?
4 What is *phrenology*?

d Discuss the questions.

1 What do you think of the different types of personality tests discussed?
2 Which ones do you think are most accurate? Least accurate?
3 Do you know anyone who has used personality tests? What did he or she use them for?

Phrenology

Written Personality Test

Personality Test

Answer the following multiple-choice questions:

Writing that slants to the right
Friendly and outgoing to other people. Often popular.

Writing that slants to the left
Less outgoing. May be shy at first.

A lot of space between words
A generous person leaves more space between words.

T's that are crossed high
Has a good self-image. Ambitious people usually cross their t's high up.

Graphology

Astrology

10 ▶ Focus on Grammar

a Look at sentences 1 and 2 and the chart below. In which sentence is the gerund used as subject?

1 Don't be nervous about taking the test.
2 Learning about personalities can be helpful for many people.

Gerunds as subjects and after prepositions	
Gerund as subject	**Studying** a person's handwriting is called "graphology." **Testing** personality is complicated.
Gerund after a preposition	Some ways **of testing** are more scientific than others. Why are people interested **in learning** about personality?

b Make sentences by matching 1–5 with a–e.

1 Add up your score after   *1e*   a working with people.
2 Taking a personality test   __   b can be good for your health.
3 The test says he's good at   __   c can help you understand yourself.
4 Doing some exercise   __   d taking a long time to finish.
5 Don't worry about   __   e answering all the questions.

c Use gerunds and make sentences. Then compare sentences with a partner.

Examples   *Eating healthy food is good for you.*   *I never worry about taking tests.*

1 _____ is / are good for you.
2 _____ isn't / aren't very good for you.
3 _____ makes me nervous.
4 I never worry about _____.

11 ▶ Vocabulary: Adjective prefixes (un-, dis-, im-)

a Read this person's handwriting analysis. Underline the personality adjectives.

> *Writing that slants to the right*
> Friendly and outgoing to other people. Often popular.

> *Writing that slants to the left*
> Less outgoing. May be shy at first.

> *A lot of space between words*
> Someone generous with time. Often leaves more space between words.

> *T's that are crossed high*
> Has a good self-image. Ambitious people usually cross their t's high up.

> *T-bar crossed with a long stroke*
> Enthusiastic: always excited about new ideas and plans.

> *Wide o's with no loops*
> Honest with their opinions. Tells the truth.

> *Sharp points on m's and n's*
> Intelligent: a quick thinker.

> *d's that are braced*
> Stubborn: it's hard to change their mind.

b **AUDIO** Try to put these words in the correct category to make negatives. Then listen and check.

friendly   organized   enthusiastic
patient   agreeable   kind   popular
intelligent   honest   polite

un-	dis-	im-
unfriendly		

c Fill in the blanks with a negative adjective.

1 The politician was _unpopular_. People didn't vote for him.
2 Lucy didn't seem to like the idea. She was _____ about it.
3 Please tell the truth. Don't be _____.
4 Can we arrange these papers? They're very _____.
5 The children were _____ because they couldn't wait for the party to begin.

12 ▶ Speaking

a Work with a partner. Look at these handwriting samples and say what you think. Use the ideas in 11a or your own ideas.

b Work in groups. Take turns presenting your thoughts to the group. How similar or different are they? Discuss your conclusions.

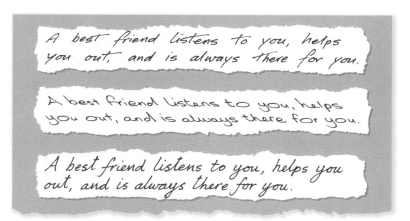

> *A best friend listens to you, helps you out, and is always there for you.*

> *A best friend listens to you, helps you out, and is always there for you.*

> *A best friend listens to you, helps you out, and is always there for you.*

13 ▸ Reading

a An "eccentric" person is someone whose behavior is unconventional or a little unusual. What do you think makes the people in these photos eccentric?

b Read the article. According to the study, what are two positive aspects of being eccentric?

Embrace Your Eccentricity

A serious study by Dr. David Weeks has discovered some very positive information for people society labels "eccentric."

The report, which has also been made into a book, concludes that eccentrics live five to ten years longer than average, and that they are usually happier, healthier, and more intelligent than the rest of us.

According to Dr. Weeks, some typical traits of eccentrics are that they are: creative, nonconforming, strongly obsessed by curiosity, idealistic, obsessed with one or more hobbies (often five or six), intelligent, opinionated, and "convinced that he or she is right and that the rest of the world is out of step."

Eccentric people are sometimes mistakenly viewed as being mildly insane. But actually, eccentrics choose to behave in an outlandish manner because it gives them positive pleasure.

The eccentrics who participated in Dr. Weeks' study also scored very well on IQ tests, where they were among the highest 15 percent of the general population.

"Eccentrics are healthier because they are happier," Dr. Weeks explains. "Stated simply, eccentrics experience much lower levels of stress because they do not feel the need to conform, and lower stress levels mean their immune systems can function more efficiently."

So if you feel like walking around in a raincoat on the hottest day of the year or shaving half of your beard off while studying underwater basket-weaving,* go for it! You're not crazy, you're eccentric, which, as it turns out, is very healthy indeed!

> * **basket-weaving** = the art of making baskets

c Read the article again. Complete the statements.

1 On average, eccentrics live _____.
2 Three examples of typical characteristics of eccentrics are _____.
3 Eccentrics act the way they do because _____.
4 Intelligence tests showed that eccentrics are _____.
5 According to Dr. Weeks, eccentrics are happier because _____.

d Find these words in the article. Choose the correct definition. (2) = paragraph number.

1 concludes (2)   ___   a seeing the world / situations as ideal
2 nonconforming (3) ___   b very strange or unusual
3 idealistic (3)   ___   c being unable to stop doing or thinking about something
4 obsessed (3)   ___   d below the surface of water
5 outlandish (4)   ___   e reaches a belief or opinion as a result of thought or study
6 underwater (5)   ___   f behaving or thinking differently from most other people in society

e What do you think about Dr. Weeks's conclusions? Do you know anyone who has some of these personality traits? Think about friends, family, acquaintances, and famous people.

14 ▶ Writing

a Think of the most interesting or unusual person you know. Then work in pairs. Interview your partner about his or her person. Ask questions to learn about personality traits that make the person interesting or unusual. Make notes of your partner's answers.

b Write a paragraph about the person your partner described. Try to include as many details as possible to show how the person is interesting or unusual.

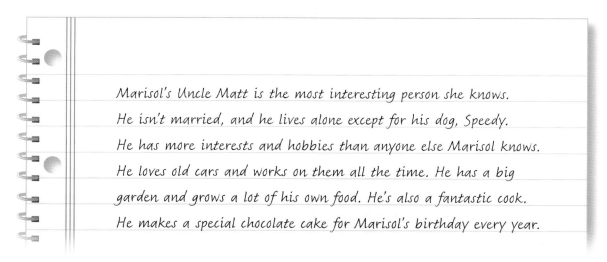

Marisol's Uncle Matt is the most interesting person she knows.
He isn't married, and he lives alone except for his dog, Speedy.
He has more interests and hobbies than anyone else Marisol knows.
He loves old cars and works on them all the time. He has a big
garden and grows a lot of his own food. He's also a fantastic cook.
He makes a special chocolate cake for Marisol's birthday every year.

c Read your descriptions. How accurate are they?

Units 4–6 Review

Grammar

1 ▸ Read the text. What can you do to help yourself remember someone's name?

"Hi. I'm, I'm, I'm . . . You'll have to forgive me, I'm terrible with names."

REMEMBERING NAMES is easier for some people. There are many ways to remember names.
I read an article a few days ago that said you should look carefully at the person you are meeting. Look for an interesting or unusual feature—long curly hair or very blue eyes—then try to find a way to connect that feature to the name. I met someone named Gloria yesterday, and she had the most *glorious* blue eyes I've ever seen. So you see, I've remembered her name…for one day anyway!

2 ▸ Complete the paragraph using the simple past or past continuous.

I ¹ *was walking* (walk) through an unfamiliar neighborhood when suddenly I ² _____ (recognize) one of the houses. The sun ³ _____ (shine), and I instantly ⁴ _____ (feel) like a child again. I ⁵ _____ (stand) there when an older woman ⁶ _____ (come) out of the house. She looked at me in surprise. "Harry, is that you?" she ⁷ _____ (ask). "I'm Mrs. Wilson…I was your babysitter!"

3 ▸ Combine the sentences using comparatives.

1 My uncle Joe is generous. My friend Ari is not very generous. (more)
   My uncle Joe is more generous than my friend Ari.
2 My apartment is big. Kate's is big, too. (as) _____
3 My sister isn't very absent-minded. I am absent-minded. (less)
   _____
4 That guitar is expensive. This guitar is not very expensive. (more)
   _____
5 My job isn't very difficult. Your job is very difficult. (as)
   _____

4 ▸ Combine the sentences using relative clauses.

1 Harry is a journalist. He wrote an article about remembering names.
   Harry is a journalist who wrote an article about remembering names.
2 Harry's wife Sandra wrote a novel. It has sold very well.
3 Harry and Sandra have a son. He is 12 years old.

5 ▸ Sandra is being interviewed. Write questions and answers using the information given. Use the simple past or present perfect simple.

Interviewer: Where were you born, Sandra?
Sandra: I was born in a small town outside of Caracas, Venezuela.
Interviewer: Really? ¹ *How long ago did you move to the United States?* (how long ago / you move / United States)
Sandra: ² _____.
(I be here / for 15 years)
Interviewer: ³ _____?
(you go / Venezuela / last year)
Sandra: No, ⁴ _____.
(I not go / Venezuela / since 1997)

6 Complete these statements with gerunds. Use your own ideas.

1 For me, _painting_ landscapes is a relaxing hobby.
2 I think that _____ is a good form of exercise.
3 I'm excited about _____.
4 I usually finish all of my work before _____.

7 Circle the correct response.

1 The phone rang while we (got / were getting) ready to go out.
2 Is the oven still on? —No, I turned (it off / off it).
3 This is the (jacket that / jacket) has a hole in it.
4 Do you ever think about (change / changing) your job?
5 Your books are everywhere! Please put (away them / them away).
6 She has worked for the same company (for / since) thirty years.

Vocabulary

8 Use the words below to make compound adjectives that complete the sentences.

**good   right   full   new   class   handed
time   brand   looking   first**

1 I am definitely _right-handed_. I can't do a thing with my left hand.
2 _____ airplane tickets cost three times more than coach tickets.
3 She only wants to work 20 hours a week—she doesn't want a _____ job.
4 Old cars are too much trouble. I want to buy a _____ one.
5 Don't you think he's _____? —Yes, he's very handsome.

9 Fill in the missing prepositions.

When you think ¹ _about_ it, friends are similar ² _____ family. They listen ³ _____ us when we are sad, they ask us ⁴ _____ our concerns, and they worry ⁵ _____ us when we are away. They are always interested ⁶ _____ our problems and are never surprised ⁷ _____ our successes. We depend ⁸ _____ friends for good advice.

Recycling Center

10 Fill in the blanks with the simple present or present continuous form of the verbs.

1 John _looks_ (look) much better than he did last week.
2 I _____ (not understand) this sentence. What does it mean?
3 Kazuo _____ (look) at the book carefully to see if it is valuable.
4 This soup _____ (taste) really good! What did you put in it?
5 I can't go to the movies with you now. I _____ (do) laundry.

Fun Spot

Write each of the words below in the correct blank to form another word.

art   and   eat   land   lip   real

s_ _lip_ _pers
out_____ish
h_____le
p_____-time
_____istic
l_____her

7 Trade and treasure

✔ Using money and exchanging services
✔ Tag questions (simple present and past); *will* vs. *be going to*

1 Listening

a Look at the movie poster and pictures. How could these items be related in a story?

b **AUDIO** Listen to the conversation. How close were your ideas to the story?

c **AUDIO** Listen again. According to the conversation, did these things happen in the movie and / or in real life? Check the correct column(s).

	Movie	Real life
1 The story is about a policeman and a waitress.	✓	✓
2 The policeman gave the waitress half of his lottery winnings.	___	___
3 The policeman knew the waitress well.	___	___
4 It was the first time the policeman went to the restaurant.	___	___
5 The policeman and the waitress chose the lottery numbers together.	___	___
6 The policeman and the waitress fell in love.	___	___

d Explain the title of the movie. Do you think it's good?

2 Vocabulary: Money

a Read the paragraph. Underline the words and expressions related to money.

The waitress worked hard, but she didn't <u>earn</u> a lot. It was difficult to save. She didn't spend a lot or waste money. She didn't buy things that she couldn't afford. Generous friends offered to lend her money, but she didn't like to borrow; she didn't want to owe them money and worry about how to pay it back.

> ▼ **Help Desk**
>
> Notice how *lend, borrow,* and *owe* are used in a sentence:
>
> *I lent a friend money.* OR
> *I lent money to a friend.*
>
> *I borrowed money from a friend.*
> (Not: *I borrowed a friend money.*)
>
> *I owe my friend ten dollars.* Or
> *I owe ten dollars to my friend.*

b Complete the conversation with the words in parentheses.

A: I don't ¹ *earn* a lot of money in my job. I try to ²_____, but it's hard. I never buy anything that I ³_____ and I try not to ⁴_____ money. I only ⁵_____ things I need.   (save / earn / buy / waste / can't afford)

B: I sometimes ¹_____ money from the bank for my business. But, I don't think it's a good idea to ²_____ money to a friend. I did it once, and he didn't ³_____ me _____. It ruined our friendship.   (pay back / lend / borrow)

3 ▶ Focus on Grammar

a Use tag questions to check information or ask for agreement. Look at the chart. Then circle the correct answers in 1 and 2.

1 In the simple present and the simple past, if the verb in the main sentence is *be*, use (*be*/*do*) in the tag. Use a form of (*be*/*do*) for other verbs.

2 If the sentence is affirmative, the tag is (affirmative/negative). If the sentence is negative, the tag is (affirmative/negative).

Tag questions: Simple present and simple past	
Affirmative sentence	**Negative sentence**
That**'s** true, **isn't** it?	That **isn't** true, **is** it?
The movie **was** based on a true story, **wasn't** it?	The movie **wasn't** based on a true story, **was** it?
That **sounds** like a Hollywood ending, **doesn't** it?	That **doesn't sound** like a Hollywood ending, **does** it?
He **gave** her half his winnings, **didn't** he?	He **didn't give** her half his winnings, **did** he?

b Match the beginnings (1–8) with the tags (a–h).

1 She's from London,   _1g_   a does he?
2 It's a beautiful day,   __   b was it?
3 You don't like to borrow money,   __   c isn't it?
4 You aren't from around here,   __   d do you?
5 They paid for dinner,   __   e weren't you?
6 Kevin doesn't like spending money,   __   f are you?
7 The bank wasn't open today,   __   g isn't she?
8 You were working yesterday,   __   h didn't they?

> ▼ **Help Desk**
>
> Short answers are often used to respond to tag questions.
>
> *That's amazing, isn't it?*
> **Yes, it is.**

c Work with a partner. Use some tag questions and make conversations for these situations.

1 the weather today or yesterday
2 a hobby or interest
3 a recent sporting event (a baseball game)
4 a movie that you've both seen

Examples A: *It's a beautiful day today, isn't it?*   C: *You like cooking, don't you?*
          B: *Yes, it is. It's nicer than yesterday.*   D: *Yes, I do. I love it. What about you?*

4 ▶ Speaking

a Look at the examples. Then write some general or personal sayings about money. Think about categories like lending and borrowing, saving, and wasting money.

b Compare your sayings as a class. How similar or different are your sayings?

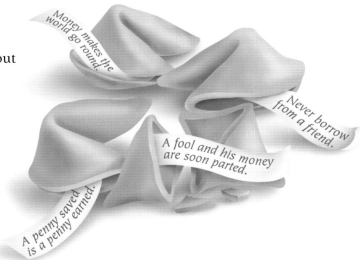

Money makes the world go round.

Never borrow from a friend.

A fool and his money are soon parted.

A penny saved is a penny earned.

5 ▸ Reading

a The woman in the photos did something surprising and generous with her life savings. Discuss what the possibilities could be. Then read the first paragraph of the article below and check your guess.

b Read the whole article. How much money has the university received in total because of Oseola McCarty's gift?

THE GIFT

Oseola McCarty spent more than 75 years washing and ironing other people's clothes. Her lined hands bear testimony to a lifetime of hard work. So, it was a surprise when Miss McCarty decided to give her entire life savings—$150,000—to the University of Southern Mississippi. Miss McCarty's gift amazed even those who thought they knew her well.

The customers who have brought their laundry and ironing to her home for more than 75 years included three generations of some families. Initially she said she charged $1.50 to $2 a bundle, but, with inflation, the price rose.

"When I started making $10 a bundle, I commenced* to save money," recalled Miss McCarty, who was born on March 7, 1908. "I put it in savings. I never would take any of it out. It just accumulated."

As her savings increased over the years, McCarty washed and ironed and lived frugally. She never learned to drive and still walks everywhere she goes. When her mother and aunt died, they each left her some money, which she added to her savings. In 1947, her uncle died and left her a modest house in which she still lives.

Until her donation, she was afraid to fly and had only been out of the South once in 50 years. Since then, she's traveled all over the country and has been the subject of many interviews and articles. She's even visited the White House and been honored by the president.

Her donation of her life savings is for students who clearly demonstrate a financial need. "I want to help somebody's child go to college," said the quiet-spoken McCarty, who left school in sixth grade and has never married or had children. "I just want it to go to someone who will appreciate it and learn. I'm old and I'm not going to live always."

Miss McCarty's generosity inspired many to give money to the university, and contributions came in from all over the country. Her gift has now been more than doubled.

In a recent magazine interview, McCarty was asked why she didn't spend the money earned over a lifetime on herself.

"I am spending it on myself," she answered, smiling.

> *** commenced** = started
> (used in formal situations)

c Read the article again. Do you think Miss McCarty would say these things or not? Write *yes* or *no*. Give reasons from the text for your answer.

1 I've always worked hard.
   Yes. The article says she did laundry for other people for more than 75 years.
2 I always charged $2 for a bundle of laundry. _____
3 I need a car. _____
4 I never travel because I'm afraid to fly. _____
5 I still have the same life I had before my donation. _____
6 I'm happy to help someone who likes learning. _____
7 Giving away money is a good thing, but first buy things for yourself.
   _____

d Find a word in the article that means the following. (2) = paragraph number.

1 a general rise in prices (2)   _____
2 increased over time (3)   _____
3 carefully, not spending a lot of money (4)   _____
4 shown great public respect (5)   _____
5 encouraged or caused to do something good (7)   _____

e What do you think is most interesting about this story? What other stories of generosity do you know?

6 ▶ Language in Action: Transactions

a **AUDIO** Listen to the two conversations. For each one, number the expressions in the order you hear them.

PAYING IN A RESTAURANT	CASHING A CHECK
___ Let me get this.	___ Can I see some identification, please?
_1_ Can we have the check, please?	___ Can I cash this check, please?
___ You paid last time.	_1_ Can I help you?
___ It's too expensive.	___ Tens, please.
___ It's my treat.	___ How would you like it? In (tens or twenties)?
___ It's / This is on me.	

b **AUDIO** Listen again. Then explain what the expressions mean.

Let me get this.   It's my treat.   How would you like it?   Tens, please.

Example   *"Let me get this" means "I want to pay for the meal."*

c Work with a partner. Practice conversations for each situation in 6a.

Example   (In a restaurant)
         A: *Can we have the check, please?*
         B: *Let me get this.*
         A: *No, you paid last time…*

RATES
4.9%
APR

7 ▶ Listening

a Look at the picture and the definition. What do you know about bartering?

b **AUDIO** Listen. How does Luke feel about bartering?

c **AUDIO** Listen again. Then discuss the questions.

1 How did Luke start to barter?
2 How does he find people to barter with?
3 Why did he have a bad experience once?
4 What are three things he has bartered for?
5 Why does he barter less now?

d What do you think about bartering? Do you know anyone who barters?

* **barter =** exchange goods or services for other goods or services, not for money

8 ▶ Vocabulary: Expressions with *make* and *do*

a Try to put the expressions with *make* or *do* into the correct diagrams. (Hint: You often use *do* with jobs or tasks and *make* with things that you create, build, or earn.)

> money   someone's hair   a profit   a mistake   a job   a living
> someone a favor   housework or chores   friends   a decision
> laundry   a list   noise   the shopping   a meal   business

make	money, _____, _____,
	_____, _____, _____,
	_____, _____, _____

do	someone's hair, _____,
	_____, _____, _____,
	_____, _____

b **AUDIO** Listen and check your answers.

c Read the information about bartering. Circle *make* or *do*.

Why barter?

Of course, you need to ¹ (make / do) money and ² (make / do) a living, but bartering can be another interesting way to get things done. You won't ³ (make / do) a profit, but it's sure to be interesting, and you may even ⁴ (make / do) some new friends in the process.

How do I get started?

Think of what you need and what you have to offer. ⁵ (Make / Do) a list. Maybe you want someone to fix something or ⁶ (make / do) chores for you. What job could you ⁷ (make / do) in return? What skill could you offer? Once you ⁸ (make / do) these decisions, start talking to people. Tell your friends what you want to do.

9 ▶ In Conversation

AUDIO What do they agree to do and when? Listen. Then read.

Chuck: What's the matter?
Sheila: There's something wrong with my air
          conditioner, and I don't know how to fix it.
Chuck: I'll take a look at it if you want.
Sheila: Really? That would be great.
Chuck: I can't do it right now because I'm going to
          have lunch, and then I have an appointment.
          But I can come back tomorrow.
Sheila: Tomorrow isn't good. I'm going to be at a
          friend's house all day. How about Sunday?
Chuck: Sure, Sunday's fine. In the afternoon?
Sheila: Yes, and then I'll buy you dinner. OK?
Chuck: OK, it's a deal. I'll call you tomorrow, and
          we can arrange the time.

10 ▶ Focus on Grammar

a Underline examples of *will* and *be going to* in the conversation above. Then circle the correct answers in 1 and 2 below.

  1 Use (*will* / *be going to*) for something that is previously planned and that you intend to do.

  2 Use (*will* / *be going to*) for something that you decide at the moment of speaking.

Future forms: *will* vs. *be going to*	
I'll take a look at it. **I'll call** you tomorrow to arrange a time.	**I'm going to be** at a friend's house tomorrow. He**'s going to fix** it on Sunday.

Note: If something is uncertain or undecided, you can use *I'm not sure, I think, maybe,* or *probably* with *will*. *I'm not sure when I'll finish work.* OR *Maybe I'll see you about 9 o'clock.*

b Fill in the blanks. Use *will* or *be going to* and the verb in parentheses.

  1 A: Why do you have all this paint?
      B: I*'m going to paint*___ (paint) my room.
      A: That's a big job. I _____ (help) you.
      B: Thanks! I'm _____ (start) on Saturday morning.
      A: OK, I _____ (come) over then.
  2 A: What _____ (you / do) today?
      B: I'm not sure. Maybe I _____ (go) to a movie or maybe I _____ (work) in the garden. Do you have plans?
      A: Yes, I _____ (meet) some friends at the beach.

c Work with a partner. Use *be going to* and *will* to talk about your plans for the next week.

  Example   A: *What are you going to do this evening?*
             B: *I'm not sure. Maybe I'll go home early. I'm a little tired.*
             A: *I'm going to see a movie. Do you want to come?*

58

11 ▶ *KnowHow*: Dealing with mistakes

a How much do you worry about making mistakes in writing and speaking? What are some mistakes you often make in grammar and vocabulary?

b Look at the strategies for dealing with mistakes. Have you tried any of them? Can you add any other ideas?

   1 Keep notes on problem points.
      For example:

- grammar points that are different in your language
- words you have problems spelling
- words that are easily confused (for example, *fun and funny*)
- irregular verbs

   2 Try to think a little before you speak.
   3 Help each other when working in pairs or groups.
   4 Check your writing carefully.

c Choose at least one strategy to use in section 12.

12 ▶ Writing and Speaking

a Think of a job or skill you have and something you want or need help with (use real jobs and skills or the ideas below). Then write a notice about it.

- fix something in your house or apartment
- help with your accounting
- do chores
- help with your computer
- babysit
- organize files
- fix a car
- clean your office
- walk your dog
- teach something (sport, cooking, language)

DO YOU WANT TO BARTER?

I'm looking for someone to trade with. Do you need help with your computer? I know a lot about computers. I can teach you about them and I can fix them too. In return, I'm looking for someone to help me clean my office and organize files. If you're interested, call me.

Call 555-9876   Call 555-9876

Call 555-9876   Call 555-9876

b Put up your notices and talk to other students. Find at least two people who can exchange something with you.

   Example **A:** *Do you need help with your computer?*
            B: *Yes, I need someone to teach me how to use it.*
            A: *I'll do that. I'm good with computers. Can you cook? I'm looking for someone to teach me to cook…*

c Work as a class. Say who you're going to barter with and what you're going to exchange.

   Example *Simon is going to teach me to play the guitar. I'm going to fix his car.*

13 ▶ Reading, Speaking, and Writing

a Look at the pictures on the flyer. What do you think "treasure" and "treasure hunting" are?

b Read the flyer. Fill in each blank with a title.

> **HOW IT WORKS   WHEN & WHERE**
> **WHAT TO BRING   WHAT   HOW MUCH**

c Find these words in the text. What do you think they mean?

> clues   solve   sharp   proceeds

d Now read the sample clues (A and B). In the picture, find the two places described in the clues below.

TREASURE IN THE CITY

Do you like solving mysteries? Do you have a clever mind? Do you know your way around the city... or want to learn more about it?

If you answered "Yes" to any of these questions—or just want to have a fun evening and meet some new people— come and join us for the sixth annual *Great Treasure Hunt!*

1 _____ : A treasure hunt to raise money for charity. The winning team receives T-shirts and the *Great Treasure Hunt* trophy.

2 *HOW IT WORKS:* You'll work in teams and get clues for places to go to around the city. Work together with your team to solve the clues and find out where to go next. The team that solves all the clues the fastest will find the treasure!

3 _____ : Saturday, March 14 at Union Plaza. Start at 5 p.m. (sharp!) and finish at 9 p.m.

4 _____ : $10 per person. All proceeds go to charity.

5 _____ : A jacket, a city map, a flashlight, water and snacks, good walking (or running!) shoes,...and a sense of adventure!

Read on for sample clues...

B
Near a place of higher learning,
The time is always changing,
Look to 9 o'clock, have a seat,
And then check underneath.

A
12, 15, 15, 11   9, 14
_ O O _   – –

20, 8, 5   6, 12, 15, 23, 5, 18, 19
T _ _   _ _ O W _ _ S

e Work in teams. Imagine you have hidden "treasure" in a public place in your area. Write at least two clues leading to the treasure. Exchange clues with other students and see if they can solve them.

8 A taste of it

✔ Agriculture, food, and industry
✔ Passive (simple present and past); *the* and quantifiers

1 Speaking and Listening

a Work with a partner. Do the quiz together and discuss your answers.

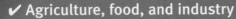

FOOD HISTORY QUIZ

How much do you know about the history of food? Take our quiz and find out!

1 The first forks were introduced in (Italy / Greece) in 1071.

2 Tea was taken to (Japan from China / China from Japan) in 1191.

3 Most of the world's tea is grown in (India / Japan).

4 Pasta was first produced commercially in (China / Italy) in 1400.

5 Chocolate was taken from (Peru / Mexico) to Spain in 1520.

6 Grapefruit trees were taken to the United States from (Portugal / Spain).

7 The first carbonated beverage* company was started in (Germany / Switzerland) in 1790.

8 Lemonade was invented in (France / the United States).

9 Most of the world's sugar is grown in (Brazil / the United States) today.

10 Most of the world's grapes are grown in (Italy / France).

* **carbonated beverage** = a drink with small bubbles, like soda

b **AUDIO** Listen and check your answers.

2 ▶ Focus on Grammar

a Look at the examples. Then circle the correct answer below.

Passive: *A lot of pasta is made in Italy.*   Active: *My grandmother makes her own pasta.*

Use the passive when the emphasis is on (the person / the process or action).

b Look at the chart. How are the simple present and simple past passive formed? Look at the quiz on page 61 again and underline the passive forms.

Passive: Simple present and simple past

Present   Tea **is grown** in India.
              Grapes **are grown** in France.
Past   Tea **was taken** to Japan from China in 1191.
              Grapefruit trees **were taken** to the United States from Spain in 1840.

Note: Use *by* if you want to name the person or thing that does the action.
*Grapes are grown **by farmers** in France.*

---

c Write passive sentences.

1 A lot of rice / grow / in China <u>*A lot of rice is grown in China.*</u>
2 Potatoes / take / to Ireland from South America in 1588 _____
3 Corn / grow / in many places in the United States today _____
4 The sandwich / invent / by the Earl of Sandwich in 1762 _____
5 The first apple trees / plant / in North America in 1629 _____
6 Today, coffee / grow / in 50 different countries _____

d Talk about products that you use. Use these ideas and verbs and make passive sentences.

food clothes cars computers   made grown produced brought taken

Example   *A lot of cars are made in Japan. My car was made in…*

3 ▶ Listening

a Look at these steps for making potato chips. Discuss what you think happens in each step.

___ cleaning and peeling   ___ weighing, packaging, and shipping
___ delivery and quality control ___ cooking and seasoning

b **AUDIO** Listen. Put the steps above in order, according to the tour guide's explanation.

c **AUDIO** Listen again and complete the chart.

POTATO CHIP STATISTICS	
Amount of potatoes used in a year to make potato chips:	_____
Amount of chips made in a year:	_____
Number of states potatoes come from:	_____
Percentage of potatoes rejected:	_____
Number of flavors available:	_____

4 ▶ Vocabulary: Food preparation and cooking

a Look at the cookbook page. Put the words into the correct category.

COOKING WORDS

| slice / chop | peel | fry | boil | roast / bake | mix | grill or barbecue |

Food preparation	Ways of cooking
slice	fry

b Complete each recipe with the words above it.

add   peel   bake   slice   mix

▼ **Help Desk**

You can use the past participle as an adjective with many of these cooking terms.

*They **fry** the potatoes.* But *I like **fried** potatoes.*

APPLE PIE

¹ _____Peel_____ 8 or 9 apples.
Then ² _____ them.
³ _____ 2 cups sugar
and 1 teaspoon cinnamon and ⁴ _____ well.
Put mixture in pie shell. ⁵ _____ in oven for
45 minutes.

mix   chop   peel   boil   add

EGG SALAD

⁶_____ 4 eggs in water. ⁷_____ the
cooked eggs and ⁸_____ them into small
pieces. ⁹_____ mayonnaise,
salt, and pepper. ¹⁰_____
well. Cover and chill.

c **AUDIO** Now listen and check your answers.

5 ▶ *KnowHow*: Consonant clusters

a **AUDIO** Listen and practice saying these words. Pay attention to the underlined sounds.

broccoli   slice   crisp   fry   grill   steam   spicy

b **AUDIO** Practice saying these foods. Then listen and check your pronunciation.

fried fish   crisp potato chips   steamed broccoli
sliced mushrooms   grilled hamburgers   spicy spaghetti

c Work with a partner. Try to make a list of other words with the consonant clusters below.
Then compare your lists with another pair.

st-, sl-, cr-, fr-, gr-, br-, sp-

6 ▶ Speaking

a Work with a partner. Imagine that you work for a TV cooking show. Think of a recipe for a favorite or unusual dish. Write a script for the TV chef to follow as he or she prepares and demonstrates the recipe. Use these questions to help you.

1 What is the dish? What ingredients are needed?
2 How is it prepared? What do you do first, next, after that…?
3 How is it served? What do you serve it with?

b Work in groups. Present your recipe and demonstration to the group. Which recipe is the easiest? Most difficult? Most unusual?

7 ▶ Language in Action: Explaining and giving reasons

a **AUDIO** Listen to the conversation. What is the fact about tea? What is the legend about tea?

b **AUDIO** Listen again. Check the expressions you hear in the chart below.

ASKING AND EXPLAINING	RESPONDING
___ Did you know that…?	___ I'd never thought of that.
___ Do you know that / how / why / where…?	___ I didn't know that.
___ That's the reason that…	___ I have no idea.
___ That's why / how…	___ That explains a lot.
___ Because of that…	
___ It's because of…that…	

c Use the expressions above to report these facts about tea.

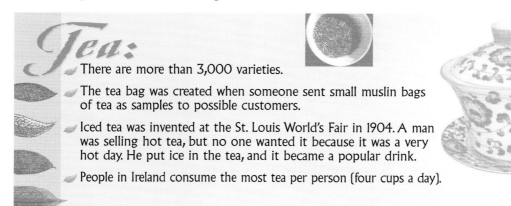

Tea:

There are more than 3,000 varieties.

The tea bag was created when someone sent small muslin bags of tea as samples to possible customers.

Iced tea was invented at the St. Louis World's Fair in 1904. A man was selling hot tea, but no one wanted it because it was a very hot day. He put ice in the tea, and it became a popular drink.

People in Ireland consume the most tea per person (four cups a day).

8 Listening

a Work in pairs or groups. Discuss how these things might all fit into a folk tale.

> a king   three daughters   presents
> salt   a prince   a wedding

b **AUDIO** Listen. What does the king learn in the story?

c **AUDIO** Listen again. Then make notes on these aspects of the story.

1 The king and his daughters:
He had three daughters, and he needed to choose one to be queen.

2 The presents: _____

3 The king's reaction: _____

4 The youngest daughter in the forest: _____

5 The wedding: _____

6 The ending: _____

d Work with a partner. Practice retelling the story in your own words. Then discuss what you think the moral of this story is.

9 Vocabulary: Common uncountable nouns

a Put the nouns into the correct category.

> information   water   furniture   mathematics   milk   love   Japanese   coffee   salt
> beauty   history   clothing   bread   honesty

General classes of objects	jewelry, mail, money, fruit, luggage, traffic, transportation, _____, _____
Liquids and solids	gas, oil, tea, shampoo, _____, _____; _____, meat, rice, pasta, cotton, wool, wood, _____, _____
Abstract nouns	advice, work, fun, luck, news, hate, _____, _____, _____, _____
Fields of study and languages	science, economics, linguistics, Spanish, _____, _____, _____

▼ **Help Desk**

Remember not to use *a / an* with uncountable nouns.
bread, advice
(Not: *a bread, an advice*)

Uncountable nouns are not usually plural.
The news was good.
(Not: *The news were good.*)

b Can you think of any other nouns to add to these categories?

10 ▶ Focus on Grammar

a Look at the chart. Circle the correct answers below.

1 (Use / Don't use) *the* in generalizations with uncountable and plural nouns.
2 (Use / Don't use) *the* when you assume the listener knows which thing you're referring to.
3 Use *a few* with (countable / uncountable) nouns.

Use of *the* and quantifiers

***Use of* the**

Generalization	*Specific reference*
Salt is necessary for life.	Can you pass *the salt*, please?
I love *music*.	Please turn down *the music*.
Books are expensive.	Put *the books* on the desk.

Quantifiers

I like *a little* salt on my food.	Jen likes *a lot of* salt on her food.
I have *a few* magazines.	My friend has *a lot of* magazines.

---

b Fill in the blanks with *the* or *N*. (*N*=nothing)

1 My favorite music is ____N____ rock music.
2 Are _____ car keys on the kitchen table?
3 Please put _____ eggs in the refrigerator.
4 My friend always gives me _____ advice when I need it.
5 Where did you put _____ sugar?
6 Olivia is studying _____ French and _____ economics.
7 There are _____ horses on my aunt's farm.

> ▼ **Help Desk**
>
> There is a difference in meaning between *little/a little* and *few/a few*.
>
> *I have little time these days.* (not much or not enough)
> *I can help you. I have a little time this afternoon.* (some)
> *We knew few people at the party.* (not many, possibly not enough)
> *We met a few interesting people at the party.* (some)

c Fill in the blanks with *a little*, *a few*, or *a lot of*.

1 We live in the country, so there's only *a little* traffic.
2 I get _____ mail every day. I don't know what to do with it all!
3 There's only _____ coffee left but enough for you and me.
4 I have _____ photographs of my friends, but I'd like more.
5 There were _____ people at the movie. It's very popular right now.
6 Could I borrow _____ of your CDs? I won't take many.

d Use these ideas (or your own) and make true sentences. Use *a little*, *a few*, *a lot of*, and *the* if necessary.

mail   books and magazines   salt on my food   coffee or tea during the day
music and CDs   pictures on my wall   experience in my work   traffic in my area

Examples   *I love books. I have a lot of books, but I only have a few magazines.*
I get a lot of mail every day. Unfortunately, the mail I get is usually junk mail.

11 ▶ Reading

a Work in pairs or groups. Make a list of things you know about ostriches. Use these questions to help you:

What do they look like? How do they behave?
Where do they live? How are they used by farmers?

b Read the article. Explain why you think the title is "Ostrich Mania."

OSTRICH MANIA

OSTRICHES ARE FUNNY-LOOKING birds. They can't fly, and they can't sing. They swallow rocks, and even diamonds if they happen to find any, to help them digest their food. They are also known for being very bad-tempered and will bite or kick their handlers if they have a chance. Their scientific name is *struthio camelus*, which means "sparrow*-camel." When travelers in the desert saw ostriches at a distance, they sometimes thought they were camels.

It seems hard to imagine that these birds would become an agricultural craze, but they did. During the late 1800s and early 1900s, ostrich farming was big business in South Africa. There was a huge demand from all over the world for ostrich feathers to decorate women's hats and clothing. Some hats were adorned with feathers more than 20 inches high. At the height of the industry in 1913, there were 750,000 ostriches in one area of South Africa producing up to 100,000 tons of feathers a year. Ostrich feathers were almost as important to the South African economy as gold, diamonds, and wool.

As is typical when people get rich quickly, there was some extravagance. The best ostriches were worth as much as some houses. Ostrich farmers became very rich and built elaborate

mansions called "feather palaces" to show off their wealth. These palaces had marble floors, many towers and balconies, and huge bathrooms.

However, with the start of World War 1, fashions changed. As a result, the demand for feathers fell quickly. Many ostrich farmers were ruined. They had to sell their mansions, and their lives changed completely.

Ostriches are still farmed today in several parts of the world, but mainly for leather and meat. The business will probably never be as big as it was during those peak years.

* **sparrow** = a small brown bird

c Read the article again. Complete the sentences with information from the article.

1 Ostriches are unusual birds because _____.
2 The scientific name for the ostrich is *Struthio camelus* because _____.
3 Ostrich farming became very big business in South Africa because _____.
4 The "feather palaces" they built were elaborate because _____.
5 The market for feathers changed very quickly because _____.

d Find the words in the text. Choose the correct definition. (1) = paragraph number.

1 swallow (1)   *1e*   a   the highest level, value, rate
2 craze (2)   ___   b   decorated in order to make more beautiful or attractive
3 adorned (2)   ___   c   try to impress people
4 show off (3) ___   d   the desire or need for something among a group of people
5 demand (4)   ___   e   make something pass from your mouth down your throat
6 ruined (4)   ___   f   a strong interest that usually only lasts for a short time
7 peak (5)   ___   g   made to lose all one's money or hope of success

e What other manias and crazes have you heard of?

12 ▶ Speaking and Writing

a Work in groups. Make a list of the things that are grown, produced, or raised in your country. Use these categories:

1 Animals and crops (chickens, sugar, rice)
2 Materials and goods (wood, cars, clothing)
3 Other (special dishes and food, music, fashion and style, attitudes)

b Imagine you're creating a publicity brochure about your country's products. Choose one product from the list you made in 12a and write a paragraph or two about it.

c Present your paragraph to another group or the class. Choose three examples that the class feels best represent your country's products.

9 By land and by sea

✔ Travel and exploration
✔ Present perfect continuous; *used to*

1 ▸ Listening: Song

a **AUDIO** Cover the song and listen. How does the singer feel about traveling?

b **AUDIO** Look at the song and listen again. Number the eight lines in the center in the correct order.

2 ▸ Speaking

a Work in groups. Look at these quotes about travel. Discuss what you think they mean. How much do you agree or disagree with each one?

"The world is a book, and those who do not travel read only a page."
—*Augustine*

"No one realizes how beautiful it is to travel until he comes home and rests his head on his old, familiar pillow."
—*Lin Yutang*

"A man travels the world over in search of what he needs and returns home to find it."
—*George Moore*

"Good company in a journey makes the way seem shorter."
—*Izaak Walton*

b How many people in the class consider themselves "travelers"? How many prefer to stay home?

On the Road Again

On the road again
Just can't wait to get on the road again
The life I love is makin' music with my friends
And I can't wait to get on the road again

On the road again
Goin' places that I've never been
Seein' things that I may never see again,
And I can't wait to get on the road again

___ And I can't wait to get on the road again
___ Insisting that the world be turning our way
___ And our way is on the road again
___ The life I love is making music with my friends
___ On the road again
___ We're the best of friends
___ Like a band of gypsies we go down the highway
___ Just can't wait to get on the road again

On the road again
Like a band of gypsies we go down the highway
We're the best of friends
Insisting that the world be turning our way
And our way
Is on the road again

3 ▶ Listening

a AUDIO Listen to the people talking about their best and worst travel experiences. Check the appropriate column and write where each experience happened.

	Good	Bad	Where did it happen?
1 **Sanjay P., Winnipeg, Canada**		✓	*at home (before the trip)*
2 **Liz K., Massachusetts, U.S.**			
3 **Marcello F., Rome, Italy**			
4 **Carmela B., New York, U.S.**			

b AUDIO Listen again. Which story is each phrase below related to? Make notes about how they're related.

1 Not understanding the language. *Story 4—didn't understand announcements, didn't change trains*

2 Hitchhiking on a very cold day. _____

3 A stolen passport. _____

4 Meeting a poet. _____

5 Canceling a business trip. _____

6 A delicious hot meal. _____

7 A very long train trip. _____

c Work with a partner. Choose one of the travel stories and retell it in your own words. Then work with students who chose other stories and take turns retelling each story.

4 ▶ Vocabulary: Travel expressions

a AUDIO Look at the words and expressions related to travel. Discuss which ones might relate to the stories in section 3. Then listen again and circle the words and expressions you hear.

to go on a (business) trip	to pack a suitcase	to buy a ticket
one-way or round-trip ticket	to take off	single or double room
to reserve a seat	to land	to check in and out
to make a reservation	to take pictures	window or aisle seat
passport	lobby	train conductor
traveler's checks	to read a map	reception desk
visa	to go sightseeing	hand luggage or carry-on bag
	to get lost	ticket counter

b Put the words and expressions from 4a into an appropriate category below.

General travel	Hotels & accommodation	Transportation

c Compare and discuss your categories. If you have different answers, explain your reasons.

5 ▶ In Conversation

AUDIO What's the problem? Listen. Then read.

Angela: I think we're lost!

Henry: Yes, I think so. I'm pretty sure we've been walking around in circles.

Angela: Well, can you tell anything from the map?

Henry: No, I can't. I've been looking at it for five minutes, and it doesn't make any sense. Let's ask someone for directions.

Angela: OK, there's someone at that bus stop.

Henry: Oh yes, we saw him about 20 minutes ago. He's been waiting for the bus since the last time we passed by here!

6 ▶ Focus on Grammar

a Look at the chart and answer the questions.

1 Is the present perfect continuous usually used for finished actions or actions continuing up to the present (especially when we say how long the action has lasted)?

2 How is the present perfect continuous formed?

Present perfect continuous

She **has been waiting** for the bus for 20 minutes.
They **haven't been waiting** very long.
How long **have** you **been waiting**?

Note: The present perfect continuous is often used with *for* or *since*, or with expressions like *recently, all day,* or *lately.*

---

b Underline two more examples of the present perfect continuous in section 5.

c Complete the paragraphs with the correct verbs in the present perfect continuous.

What have Elaine and Josh been doing recently?

Elaine: We ¹ *'ve been traveling* for two months now. It's great! We ² _____ things that we never do at home. I ³ _____ to learn some Spanish, but I can't speak that well yet. My husband ⁴ _____ about every place we visit, so we're learning a lot on this trip. (do / travel / try / read)

Josh: Not much. I ⁵ _____ a lot. We have a big project to do, so I ⁶ _____ to work early and I ⁷ _____ late. I ⁸ _____ enough, so I'm tired. (not sleep / finish / work / get)

d Ask and answer questions with a partner about what you have or haven't been doing lately.

work and job   **family and friends**   **sports and hobbies**   **studying**

Example   **A:** *What have you been doing lately?*
          B: *I've been working a lot. I haven't been going out with friends because…*

7 ▷ Language in Action: Travel arrangements

a **AUDIO** Listen. What are the people doing in each situation? What change does each traveler make?

b **AUDIO** Listen again. Number the expressions in the order you hear them.

HOTEL RECEPTION	AIRLINE TICKET COUNTER
___ Can you fill out this form, please?	___ Here's your new ticket.
___ How many nights are you staying?	___ When would you like to fly?
___ Here are your keys.	___ Is it possible to change my flight?
___ I have a reservation.	___ There's a flight at (time) on (date).
___ Can I have your credit card, please?	___ There's a (amount) charge to change this ticket.

c Work with a partner. Use the expressions from 7b and practice a conversation at a hotel reception desk. Then change partners and practice a conversation at an airline ticket counter.

A = Hotel or airline clerk   B = Customer

A: Greet customer.

A: Respond.

A: Respond and give more information.

B: Say why you're there.

B: Ask for a change (either room type or date of flight).

B: End the conversation politely.

8 ▷ Writing

a Think of your most interesting travel story. Write a paragraph for a "Travelers' Stories" book.

> *My best travel experience was when I was traveling in Florida with some friends. We were staying in a hotel near the beach....*

b Work with a partner and take turns. A, read your story. B, ask questions about points that are not clear to you. Make suggestions if you notice any mistakes. Then switch. After that, rewrite your stories to prepare for "publication." Add details to make your story more interesting.

9 ▸ Reading

A

Today's Book Review:
8 MEN AND A DUCK

8 Men and a Duck, by Nick Thorpe, is the story of an unlikely adventure at sea. Thorpe, a journalist, joins a crew of seven other men (and a pet duck!) to travel from northern Chile to Easter Island in a reed boat made by hand.

Thorpe joined the group purely by chance. He was traveling by bus in Bolivia when he met another crew member. At first, he only wanted to write a story about the trip, but instead, he decided to join the crew.

What makes this different from other adventure travel stories is the incredible lack of experience and expertise of the crew. The international group—Bolivian, Chilean, French, North American, and Scottish—had very little sailing experience. They couldn't even turn the boat around!

All this makes for an unusual and very entertaining travel book. Highly recommended!

B

8 MEN AND A DUCK

I woke in the darkness, sleepy yet anxious, to a sound I couldn't place. The usual noise of the cabin had stopped. Instead came a kind of muffled roar.

Holding back fear, I checked for familiar reference points: my glasses hanging near me, my life jacket used as a pillow, my safety harness at the end of the bed. It was 1:30 a.m. I lay there feeling my body move against the safety rope.

The door to the cabin opened. Rain. Torrential rain. "Everybody up! We have an emergency!" shouted Phil. Our captain's voice sounded different—tight, not as relaxed as usual.

I stepped outside. The *Viracocha* was a mess. The sails were up against the wrong side of the mast.

I went to find Erik, our Bolivian boat-builder. He was on the other side of the boat. "Not good" he murmured. "The boat's already sunk a foot lower than when we left." he said, "But now the rain will soak the reeds from above too. If it rains like this for much longer we may be too low in the water to continue."

Meaning what exactly? We would sink? I looked at the waterline... and decided not to ask any more questions.

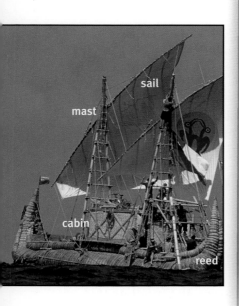

sail

mast

cabin

reed

a Read the book review (A). What kind of trip does the book describe? Is the review positive or negative?

b Read the review again. Answer questions 1 and 2.

1 How did Nick Thorpe become part of the crew?   2 What was special about the crew?

c Look at pictures from *8 Men and a Duck*. What other information do they give you about the boat and the voyage?

d Read the excerpt (B) quickly. What kind of situation are they in?

e Read the excerpt again. Answer the questions.

1 What did Nick hear when he woke up? _____
2 What was the weather like? _____
3 What did Phil, the Captain, say? _____
4 What was wrong with the boat? _____
5 What was Erik worried about? _____

f Look at the excerpt again. Make a list of vocabulary related to these topics.

1 The boat and equipment: _____
2 The weather: _____
3 People's feelings: _____

g Would you like to read this book? Give reasons for your answer.

10 ▶ Vocabulary: Prepositions and nouns

a Look at the sentences. Add the examples to the diagrams.

The reed boat was made *by* hand.
Nick Thorpe joined the expedition *by* chance.
He was traveling *by* bus *in* Bolivia.
The computer didn't work so the crew couldn't stay *in* touch *by* e-mail.
They communicated *by* satellite phone.
The story was *on* the radio and *in* the newspaper.

by	plane, taxi, accident, mistake, ___, ___, ___, ___, ___

on	TV, strike, vacation, purpose, ___

in	a magazine, ___, ___, ___

b Work with a partner. Cover the nouns in the diagrams. How many prepositions and nouns can you put together?

Example   A: *on*
          B: *on vacation, on the radio*

11 ▶ Listening

a Can you name any famous explorers from the past? What do you think some of the difficulties of early exploration were?

b **AUDIO** Listen. Does Annelise believe modern exploration is more or less difficult than early exploration? Does she believe people will continue to explore?

c **AUDIO** Listen again. Discuss the questions.

1 What is one activity Annelise has done?
2 When did she get interested in exploration?
3 What does she say about early women explorers?
4 Give two differences between early and modern exploration.

d What modern explorers do you know of?

12 ▶ Focus on Grammar

a Look at the chart. Then circle the correct answer and answer the question.

1 *Used to* describes situations, regular actions, or routines in the (past, present).
2 How are questions and negative statements formed?

> **Used to**
>
> I **used to** read about famous explorers when I was a child.
> They **used to** travel with heavy clothes and equipment.
> They **didn't use to** have the equipment we have now.
> How **did** people **use to** travel?
>
> ---
>
> **Note:** You can use *used to* to express both habits and states in the past.
> *We used to go to the mountains for our summer vacation.* (habit)
> *My family used to have a cabin in the mountains.* (state)

b Write sentences using *used to / didn't use to*.

1 People / travel on horseback
   People used to travel on horseback.
2 They / not / travel by plane
   _____
3 Women / wear long dresses
   _____
4 Trips / take much longer
   _____

c Work with a partner. Tell your partner how the situations below have changed for you.

**daily routines   job   appearance
accomodations   friends   hobbies and entertainment**

Example *I used to sleep late on weekends. I didn't use to like getting up early, but now I do.*

13 ▸ *KnowHow*: Improving fluency

> **fluency** = the ability to speak a language smoothly, easily, and well

a Look at the definition and discuss the questions.

1 Are there situations where you speak more or less fluently in English?
2 What are some specific obstacles to fluency?

b Look at the situations and the strategies for fluency (1–6). Discuss which strategies might be most useful in each situation.

**buying something in a store or hotel   talking with friends at a party
making a presentation in class   introducing yourself at a business conference**

1 Use topics and vocabulary that you know.
2 Plan or think about what you want to say beforehand.
3 Don't be afraid to make mistakes when you speak.
4 If you don't know a word, try to explain it or use a substitute word.
5 Don't be afraid to pause and take time to think while speaking.
6 Practice as much as possible! Try to find opportunities to speak.

c Try to practice some of the strategies in the next section.

14 ▸ Speaking

a Work in pairs or small groups. Imagine you are travel agents. Create an interesting trip to offer your customers and prepare a presentation to advertise it. Use these questions to help you.

1 What kind of trip is it: adventurous, educational…?
2 What's the destination?
3 What are the food and accommodations like?
4 How many people will travel together?
5 How long is the trip? What is the price of the trip?

b Present your trip to other groups or the class. Which trip would each student like to take? Is there a trip that is most popular?

76

Grammar

1 Read the text. What "treasure" did the farmer find? What will he do with it?

FARMER FINDS "TREASURE" Harold Hammond, a farmer, has found "buried treasure" in his barn—an old wooden table. After it was cleaned up, experts agreed that the table was worth about half a million dollars, so Harold decided to sell it. "My family needs the money, and I don't care about the table. I didn't even know I had it, did I? I'm going to buy new equipment for myself and my neighbors, and pay off some debts," he says. "My neighbors and I have been having a hard time. Now I can help. I know this is the right thing to do."

2 Complete the conversation with tag questions and short answers.

Interviewer: Welcome, radio listeners. We are talking to Anna Lee, of Scranton, Pennsylvania. Ms. Lee, you're Harold's neighbor, ¹ *aren't you*_____?

Anna: Yes, ²_____. And I'm very lucky to be one of them, too.

Interviewer: He's a very generous man, ³_____?

Anna: Yes, ⁴_____. He's always been a good neighbor.

Interviewer: But you didn't expect this kind of help from him, ⁵_____?

Anna: No, ⁶_____. I mean, we didn't know he had that kind of money in his barn, ⁷_____?

3 Complete the responses. Use *will* or *be going to.*

1 I can't carry this by myself!
   —I _'ll_ help you.

2 Have you made an appointment with Mr. Wilson?
   —Yes, I _____ see him tomorrow at three.

3 What are Maria's plans?
   —She _____ spend the summer in São Paulo.

4 How are you getting to New York?
   —We _____ probably drive.

4 Rewrite the sentences in the passive.

1 They don't steam vegetables in this restaurant—they grill them.
   Vegetables aren't steamed in this restaurant—they are grilled.

2 In Latin America, they often make corn into flour for tortillas and other dishes.
   _____

3 In the past they grew apples and pears in Harold's area, but now they grow wheat.
   _____

4 The bakery made the cakes for the party two days ago.
   _____

5 Circle the correct expressions.

1 I'm going to plant (a few / a little) flowers.

2 Are (tomatoes / the tomatoes) vegetables?

3 (The tomatoes / Tomatoes) that came from Jack's garden are delicious.

4 Because of the weather, they only grew (a few / a little) rice last year.

5 (Corn / The corn) needs a lot of sun to grow well.

6 Fill in the blanks with the verbs in parentheses. Use the present perfect continuous.

Takeshi: Hi, Daria! What a mess! All the flights are delayed. [1] *Have you been waiting* (you / wait) long?

Daria: I [2]_____ (sit) here for four hours.

Takeshi: Oh dear. What [3]_____ (you / do)?

Daria: I [4]_____ (not / do) much. I [5]_____ (just / look) at this book about the antiques business. I [6]_____ (think) about opening my own shop.

7 Complete the paragraph with the appropriate forms of *used to* and the verbs in parentheses.

When I was a child, we [1] *used to travel* (travel) a lot. We [2]_____ (go) to Australia, Europe, and Asia very often, and we even went to Africa once. I [3]_____ (enjoy) seeing new places, and in every country we went to I tried to learn some of the language and customs. It [4]_____ (not bother) me that I couldn't speak to the other children right away. I just listened carefully and copied what they said.

Now write three more questions with *used to* that are answered in the text.

What did the writer use to do when he was a child?

_____

_____

_____

_____

_____

Vocabulary

8 Fill in the blanks with the words below.

by   experience   on   reservation   lend

1 OK, I can _____ you twenty dollars, but you have to pay it back next week.

2 She hates flying, so she always tries to travel _____ boat or train.

3 I'd like to make a _____ for the six o'clock flight to Bogota.
— I'm sorry, ma'am, that flight is full.

4 You need a good education and a lot of _____ to be a good manager.

5 I am going to be _____ vacation next week, so call me the week after.

Recycling Center

9 Put the verbs in parentheses into the present perfect simple or simple past.

Dan Ruey is a wonderful guy. I [1] *have known* (know) him for many years. We [2]_____ (meet) when we [3]_____ (be) students, and we [4]_____ (be) good friends since then. When he [5]_____ (come) to the United States from China he [6]_____ (not know) anyone here. I [7]_____ (be) his first real friend, and that [8]_____ (be) a bond between us ever since.

Fun Spot

Find seven words that have to do with ways of preparing food. The words go in all directions.

S	T	E	A	M	G	R
T	L	E	E	P	R	O
A	M	I	X	B	I	A
R	X	R	C	C	L	S
Y	B	D	K	E	L	T
R	A	D	B	O	I	L
F	F	A	O	L	D	K

10 Hard to believe?

✔ Beliefs and first impressions
✔ First conditional; advisability: modals and expressions

1 ▶ Listening

a Take one minute and make a list of as many sports as you can think of. Compare your list with a partner. Then say what you know about the sports in the photos.

b **AUDIO** Listen to the news story. Number the sports in the order you hear them. How is a coin part of the story?

c **AUDIO** Listen again. Which sports are items 1–6 associated with? Are they supposed to be good luck or bad luck?

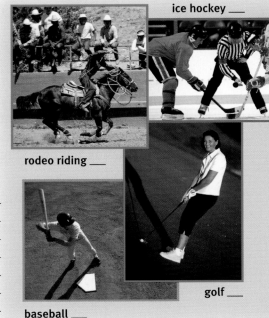

ice hockey ___

rodeo riding ___

golf ___

baseball ___

1 a buried coin	*ice hockey—good luck*
2 gum on your hat	_____
3 a dog walking across the field	_____
4 wearing yellow	_____
5 a hat on the bed	_____
6 carrying coins (x2)	_____
	_____

d What do you think of this news story? Have you ever heard of any of these superstitions?

2 ▶ Vocabulary: Easily confused verbs

a Look at the words in italics. Work with a partner and answer the questions.

1 *use / wear / carry*: Which verb is most typically used with: clothes? / a bag? / a computer?
2 *take / bring*: Which verb is usually used for something that comes toward you? Which one is usually used for something that goes away from you?
3 *win / earn*: Which verb is used for races and competitions? Which is used for money you get for working?
4 *lose / miss*: Which verb means not to catch, hit, or see something? Which means you can't find something?
5 *look at / watch*: Which verb is used for something that is changing or developing as you observe it?
6 *meet / know*: Which verb is used for the first time you are introduced to someone?

b Circle the correct verb.

1 Soccer players usually (wear / carry / use) a special uniform.
2 I (knew / met) my girlfriend at a basketball game.
3 She's looking for a different job to (win / earn) more money.
4 Let's go! If we don't hurry, we'll (miss / lose) the start of the game.
5 Could you please (bring / take) my jacket to the cleaners?
6 We stayed to (watch / look at) the end of the game, but our team lost.

3 ▶ Focus on Grammar

a Look at the chart. Circle the correct option and answer the questions.

1   In the first conditional, use the (simple present / future) in the *if* clause.
2   Is it possible to change the order of clauses in a conditional sentence? When do you use a comma?

First conditional	
If *clause*	***Main clause***
If you **put** gum on your hat,	you**'ll have** good luck.
If you **put** your hat on a bed,	you **might get** injured.
If you **wear** yellow,	you**'ll have** bad luck.
If you **carry** coins in your pocket,	you **won't win** a lot of money.

Note: It's possible to use other future forms besides *will*. For example, *might, could, be going to. If we win the game, we're going to celebrate.*
The order of the clauses can be reversed. *You'll have bad luck if you wear yellow.*

b Make sentences using the first conditional.
(Note: The *if* clause isn't always first.)

> **▼ Help Desk**
>
> Remember not to use a future form, for example *will*, in the *if* clause.
>
> *If we win the game,…*
> (Not: *If we will win the game,…*)

1   carry coins in your pocket / have a good game (golf)
If you carry coins in your pocket, you'll have a good game.
2   not have good luck / step on the court lines (tennis)
_____
3   wear the same clothes / continue winning (bowling)
_____
4   wear double numbers on your uniform / have good luck (football)
_____
5   hold more than two balls when serving / not serve well (tennis)
_____
6   have a good game / wipe the bottoms of your shoes (basketball)
_____

c Explain other superstitions you know related to sports or other activities.

Example *For golf, they say, "If it's raining when you start, you'll have a good game."*

d Work in groups. Make sentence chains. Each person adds another possibility to the chain. See how long you can go!

If it rains tomorrow,…	If I'm tired this evening,…
If the weather is nice this weekend,…	If I work (or study) hard,…

Example   A: *If it rains tomorrow, I won't walk to work.*
              B: *If I don't walk to work, I'll take the bus.*
              C: *If I take the bus, I'll…*

Language in Action: Saying what you believe or don't believe

a [AUDIO] Listen to the conversation. What does the "parking tiger" do, according to Michele?

b [AUDIO] Listen again. Check the expressions you hear in the conversation.

SAYING YOU BELIEVE SOMETHING	SAYING YOU DON'T BELIEVE SOMETHING
___ I really believe (that)…	___ That can't be true.
___ I'm positive (that)…	___ Oh, come on!
___ I always think (that)…	___ Do you expect me to believe that?
___ I have no doubt (that)…	___ That's too much!
___ It's (really) true.	___ I don't believe it.
___ It (really) works.	

c Work with a partner and make your own conversations. Use expressions from above and these ideas (or your own) about things that might or might not be true.

**a full moon affects people's behavior   loud music makes you more aggressive
chicken soup cures a cold   some people are luckier than others**

Example A: *I'm positive that a full moon affects how people act.*
              B: *That's too much! A full moon can't affect people like that.*
              A: *I really believe it's true. People act differently when there's a full moon…*

Writing and Speaking

a Write a short description of a lucky charm you use, or a little superstition you have. (Or write why you don't have any.) <u>Don't</u> put your name on your description.

> *When I watch my favorite soccer team on TV, I always watch with my friend Rafael. We each sit in the same chairs every time we watch. I wear a T-shirt in the team colors*

b Work in groups. One person (or the teacher) reads the descriptions. See if you can guess who each description belongs to.

6 ▶ Listening: Song

a AUDIO Cover the song and listen. What is the magic the singer believes in? What causes it?

b AUDIO Circle these words in the song. Then listen again and put each word in the correct column in the chart. In two-syllable words, look at the underlined vowel sound.

believe	makes	face	late
in	tell	feet	then
mag<u>i</u>c	rhythm	seem	set
free	l<u>i</u>sten	m<u>ay</u>be	

/ i /	/ ɪ /	/ eɪ /	/ ɛ /
bel<u>ie</u>ve	in	makes	tell

7 ▶ *KnowHow*: Common vowel sounds

a AUDIO Listen. Notice the difference in vowel sounds in each pair.

	/ i /	/ ɪ /		/ eɪ /	/ ɛ /
1	feet	fit	5	late	let
2	leave	live	6	tale	tell
3	feel	fill	7	gate	get
4	sheep	ship	8	taste	test

b AUDIO Now listen and underline the word you hear in each pair above.

c Work with a partner. Say one word from each pair. Your partner circles the correct word.

Do You Believe in Magic

Do you believe in magic
in a young girl's heart,
how the music can free her
whenever it starts,
and it's magic
if the music is groovy
and makes you feel happy
like an old-time movie?
I'll tell you 'bout the magic
and it'll free your soul,
but it's like try'n to
tell a stranger 'bout
a-rock 'n' roll.

If you believe in magic,
don't bother to choose
if it's jug band music
or rhythm and blues,
just go and listen
'n' it'll start with a smile
that won't wipe off your face
no matter how hard you try.
Your feet start tappin'
and you can't seem to find
how you got there,
so just blow your mind.

If you believe in magic,
come along with me.
We'll dance until mornin'
'til it's just you and me,
and maybe,
if the music is right,
I'll meet you tomorrow
so late at night,
and we'll go dancin',
baby, then you'll see
how the magic's in the music
and the music's in me!
Yeah.

Do you believe in magic?
Yeah!
Believe in the magic of a
    young girl's soul,
believe in the magic of
    a-rock and roll,
believe in the magic that
    can set you free.
Oh, talkin' 'bout the magic.
I believe.
Do you believe like I believe.
Do you believe like I believe.

82

8 ▸ Reading

a Look at the photos of smiles. What is different about each smile?

b Read the article quickly. Choose the best summary.

a People often use facial expressions, but never facial shape, to try to learn about people.
b People often use facial expressions and facial shape to try to learn about people.

Reading Faces

An old proverb says, "You can't judge a book by its cover." This means that you can't tell what people are like just by looking at them. But, most people feel they can learn some things from reading someone's face. If nothing else, they try to read people's faces to tell how they are feeling at a given moment.

Consider the smile. It is one of the most easily recognizable human facial expressions. We can see a smile on someone's face from hundreds of feet away. But, there is a subtle difference between a genuine smile and a false one. For example, when two old friends meet, they smile with their eyes as well as with their lips. The muscles of the face contract and pull the lips up, while the muscles around the eyes wrinkle the skin around the corners of the eyes. On the other hand, when a clerk in a grocery store smiles politely, the lips move but the smile doesn't necessarily reach the eyes.

We may be able to read common emotions like joy, sadness, and anger from facial expressions, but that's not all. Research suggests that we also tend to judge character, and even stereotype people, based on the shape of their faces. In her book *Reading Faces*, Professor Leslie Zebrowitz documents her research showing that baby-faced adults (people with big eyes and round cheeks) make the rest of us feel protective, as we do towards children. In one study of cases in a Boston courtroom, Zebrowitz found that people with "baby faces" were more likely to be successful than people with more mature-looking faces.

So, it might be a good idea to think twice the next time you have a quick impression of someone. Your assumptions may or may not be true!

c Read the article in 8b again. Write T (true), F (false), or NI (no information).

1 People often try to look at faces to learn how someone feels. __
2 A smile is one of the easiest expressions for people to see. __
3 A false smile uses muscles near the eyes, but a real smile does not. __
4 Adults and children are equally good at reading faces. __
5 Professor Zebrowitz found that people react in a specific way to "baby-faced" people. __
6 In the study of court cases, people with mature-looking faces were more successful. __
7 There are many books on the subject of face reading. __

d Find the words in the article. Choose the correct definition. (1) = paragraph number.

1 proverb (1)   _1g_   a cause something to have thin folds or lines in it
2 subtle (2)   __   b things you accept as true even though you have no proof
3 genuine (2)   __   c make or become shorter or smaller
4 contract (2)   __   d wanting to keep someone safe
5 wrinkle (2)   __   e real
6 stereotype (3)   __   f not very noticeable
7 protective (3)   __   g a short saying stating a general truth or piece of advice
8 assumptions (4) __   h have a fixed idea about something which is often not true in reality

e What do you think of the ideas in the article? In what situations do you think people are most / least likely to judge someone based on appearance?

9 ▶ In Conversation

AUDIO What are Martin and Rita talking about? Do they agree? Listen. Then read.

Martin: I think I'd better get a new suit for my job interview.

Rita: But a new suit is expensive. Why don't you just wear the one you have?

Martin: Well, a new suit will make a better impression.

Rita: Come on. They won't judge you on what you're wearing.

Martin: Well, they're not supposed to, but they will.

Rita: Well, I think you ought to wear what you have.

Martin: Hmm, maybe you're right. I'll think about it.

Rita: OK. Now, let's talk about what they might ask at the interview. That's what you should think about!

10 ▷ Focus on Grammar

a Look at the chart and answer these questions.

1 Which expressions use *to*? Which don't?   2 How is the negative formed for each one?

> **Advisability: Modals and expressions**
>
> | | |
> |---|---|
> | *For general advice* | You **ought to / should / shouldn't** get a new suit. |
> | *For strong or urgent advice and warnings (often directed at ourselves)* | **I'd better** leave now or I'll be late! You**'d better not** be late! |
> | *For general beliefs; what people expect or should do according to rules or law* | You**'re supposed to** arrive at 9:00 a.m. They**'re not supposed to** judge you on what you wear. |
>
> **Note:** *Ought to* is not used in negatives and questions.
> *Had better* is not used in questions.

b Fill in each blank with an appropriate expression.

supposed to / start   ought to / try   had better (not) / touch
should / do   had better / see   (not) supposed to / park

1 I feel tired all the time. What <u>should I do</u>?
2 Look at the "No Parking" sign. You _____ here.
3 You _____ that new Thai restaurant. It's great!
4 You _____ that pan. It's really hot.
5 Where is everyone? The meeting _____ right now.
6 You've had a fever for a week. You _____ a doctor!

c Write some advice for these situations. Then compare and discuss your advice with a partner.

1 You think your friend worries about his or her appearance too much.
2 Your friend never follows rules when driving. He or she drives too fast, parks anywhere, etc.

11 ▷ Listening

a **AUDIO** Listen to two different people talking about mistaken first impressions. What was not true in each case?

b **AUDIO** Listen again. Which story does each piece of information below go with? Explain the significance of each one.

<u>2</u> a drive in the country   ___ she wasn't very friendly   ___ she started laughing
___ a new boss   ___ "Give me your keys"   ___ more responsibility
___ a flat tire   ___ dropped files and spilled coffee ___ "Go home"
___ a gang of men   ___ changed the tire   ___ a good friend now

c What do you think of these stories? Has anything similar ever happened to you?

12 Vocabulary: Phrasal verbs

a **AUDIO** Look at the phrasal verbs. Listen to the stories again. Mark the phrasal verbs you hear.

Story 1		Story 2	
1 __	*take over*	1 __	*pull over*
2 __	*pick up*	2 __	*get in / into*
3 __	*sit down*	3 __	*get out of*
4 __	*stand up*	4 __	*get on*
5 __	*take on*	5 __	*get off*
		6 __	*give back*

> **Glossary**
>
> **take over** = take control of or responsibility for (a job or position)
>
> **take on** = accept or decide to do something
>
> **pull over** = move to the side of a road
>
> **give back** = return something to someone

b Replace the underlined words with the correct form of a phrasal verb.

1 Please <u>have a seat</u>, and we'll start the meeting. *sit down*
2 Monica didn't want to <u>leave</u> the bus because it was raining. _____
3 Can you <u>return</u> my CD, please? _____
4 The car was making a funny noise, so we <u>moved to the side of the road</u>. _____
5 A new company is <u>taking control of</u> ours. There may be a lot of changes. _____

c Choose one of the stories from section 11. Work with someone who chose the other story. Practice retelling the stories, using as many of the phrasal verbs as you can.

13 Speaking and Writing

a Work with a partner. Think of a situation where your first impression of someone or something either changed a lot or was completely correct. Use the following questions to help you. Then tell your partner about the situation.

—Think about how or when you met someone (a friend, co-worker, boss, etc.). What first impressions did you have? Were your impressions correct?
—Think about the first time you visited a place (your school, a new home, etc.). How did you feel about it?

b Write a paragraph about your example. Describe how your impression changed or didn't change and why.

c Work in groups. Compare your stories. How many are about <u>incorrect</u> first impressions and how many are about <u>correct</u> first impressions? What conclusions can you draw from this?

11 Down to earth

✔ The physical and animal worlds
✔ Modal verbs for possibility; reported requests
   ask, tell, and *want*

1 ▶ Speaking

a Work with a partner. Look at the landscape pictures. Which scene do you like the most? Which do you like the least? Why?

b Compare answers as a class. Is there a natural setting that most people prefer?

2 ▶ Vocabulary: Geography

a Look at the words below. For each word, find the corresponding number in the photos above.

> mountain (mountain range) (1)   forest (2)   hill (3)
> valley (4)   desert (5)   river (6)   lake (7)   ocean (8)
> coast (9)   rainforest (10)   waterfall (11)   island (12)

b Give a specific example for each word in 2a.

> Example   mountain range: *the Andes*

▼ Help Desk

Use *the* with names of:

—oceans and seas:
   the Pacific Ocean

—deserts: *the Sahara*

—mountain ranges: *the Himalayas*

—rivers: *the Nile*

—island groups: *the West Indies*

Listening

a AUDIO Listen to the conversation. What is the main topic?

1 Plants and gardening
2 Nature and health
3 People and hospitals

b AUDIO Listen again. Discuss the questions.

1 What kind of research is the professor doing?
2 What two research studies does Stuart mention?
3 Why does Ben believe gardening is good for him?

c What do you think of the ideas discussed in the conversation?

Focus on Grammar

a Look at the chart. Which modal verb(s) can you use for…

1 something that you think is possible, but you don't know for sure? _____
2 something that you're almost sure is <u>not</u> true or <u>not</u> possible? _____
3 something that you're almost sure is true? _____

Modals: Possibility (speculation)

Contact with nature **may / might / could** have health benefits. Scientists aren't sure yet.
Gardening **must** be good for me. It always makes me feel calmer.
It **can't** be true. There's no evidence for it.

Note: Use *could*, not *may* or *might*, to speculate with *yes /no* questions.
For example: *Could it have health benefits?*

---

b Fill in the blanks with a modal verb. (More than one answer is possible in some cases.)

1 Where's Louise?   —I'm not sure. She _____ be in the garden.
2 Isn't that Ben over there?   —No, it _____ be him. He's in Italy until next week.
3 I can't find my mug.   —It _____ be on the table, or it _____ on the desk.
4 I'm really hungry.   —You _____ be hungry. We just finished dinner!
5 Those plants don't look   —They _____ need water. They haven't been watered
   very healthy.   in days!

c Use *may, might, could, must,* and *can't* to
speculate about the painting.

Examples *That must be a mountain.*
That might be a river.

5 ▶ Reading

a Look at the photo of Curtis Ebbesmeyer and read the introduction to the article about an unusual oceanographer. What are some possible answers to the question in the introduction?

Athletic shoes, plastic bathtub toys, and a group of beachcombers on the northwestern coast of the United States.

How are these things all a part of a serious scientific study of oceans and ocean currents?

b Read the article quickly. Check your guesses.

Scientists today are studying ocean currents more and more intensely. Most do it using satellites and other high-tech equipment. However, oceanographer Curtis Ebbesmeyer does it in a more old-fashioned way—by studying movements of random junk*.

A scientist with many years' experience, he started this type of research in the early 1990s when he heard about hundreds of athletic shoes washing up on the shores of the northwest coast of the United States. There were so many shoes that people were holding swap meets to try and match left and right shoes to sell or wear.

Ebbesmeyer started investigating and found out that the shoes—about 60,000 in total—fell into the ocean in a shipping accident. He contacted the shoe company and asked if they wanted the shoes back. Not surprisingly, the company told him that they didn't. Ebbesmeyer realized this could be a great experiment. If he learned when and where the shoes went into the water and tracked where they landed, he could learn a lot about the patterns of ocean currents.

The Pacific Northwest is one of the world's best areas for beachcombing because of converging winds and currents, and as a result, there is a group of serious beachcombers in the area. Ebbesmeyer got to know a lot of them and asked for their help in collecting information about where the shoes landed. In a year he collected reliable information on 1,600 shoes. With this data, he and a colleague were able to test and refine a computer program designed to model ocean currents, and publish the results of their study.

Then in 1993, a shipment of colored plastic bathtub toys fell into the North Pacific ocean. Ebbesmeyer and his colleagues got even more accurate information from this spill, which resulted in huge amounts of useful new data for their work.

As the result of his work, Ebbesmeyer has become known as the scientist to call with questions about any unusual objects found floating in the ocean. He has even started an association of beachcombers and oceanographers, with 500 subscribers from West Africa to New Zealand. They have documented spills of everything from onions to hockey gloves.

* **junk** = old, useless things

c Read the article again. Answer the questions.

1 What is different about the way Curtis Ebbesmeyer studies ocean currents?
2 How did he get started doing this kind of research?
3 How did he use the athletic shoes for research?
4 How are beachcombers a part of his work?
5 Why were the bathtub toys very helpful for his work?
6 How many people are part of his association, and what have they done?

d How important do you think this kind of work is? Do you know of any other unusual scientific studies on the natural world?

6 ▶ Vocabulary: Prepositions of movement

a How many pairs of opposites can you make with the prepositions below?

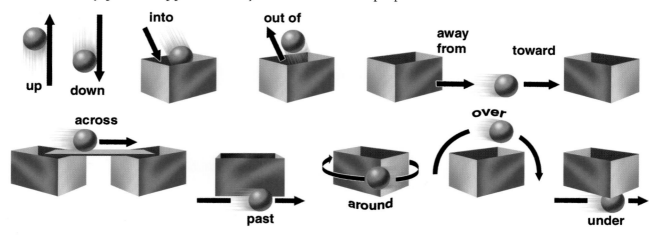

b Find the Kuroshio Current on the diagram. Read the description, check the path on the diagram, and choose the correct prepositions.

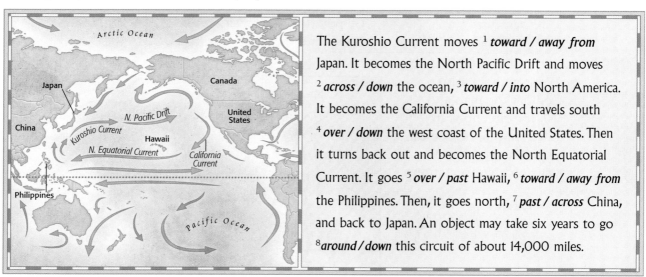

The Kuroshio Current moves ¹ *toward / away from* Japan. It becomes the North Pacific Drift and moves ² *across / down* the ocean, ³ *toward / into* North America. It becomes the California Current and travels south ⁴ *over / down* the west coast of the United States. Then it turns back out and becomes the North Equatorial Current. It goes ⁵ *over / past* Hawaii, ⁶ *toward / away from* the Philippines. Then, it goes north, ⁷ *past / across* China, and back to Japan. An object may take six years to go ⁸ *around / down* this circuit of about 14,000 miles.

c Work with a partner. Take turns describing other currents on the diagram.

90

Language in Action: Directions

a **AUDIO** Is it possible to get to the trail they want? Listen. Then read.

Hiker 1: Hi!

Hiker 2: Hi. Can you help us? We wanted to go to the Windy Lake Trail, but I think ¹ *we're lost* .

Hiker 1: You ² _____. It's ³ _____.

Hiker 2: Oh, no! Another hiker told us to come up this trail.

Hiker 1: It happens a lot. It's a little confusing.

Hiker 2: Can we get to the trail from here?

Hiker 1: Well, you could ⁴ _____. Or, you can just ⁵ _____. This trail crosses the Windy Lake Trail.

Hiker 2: So we can just ⁶ _____ this trail?

Hiker 1: Yes, ⁷ _____ the trail for about a mile. ⁸ _____ the lake. You'll see a sign for the Windy Lake Trail just before the lake.

Hiker 3: Thank you very much.

Hiker 1: No problem. Enjoy your hike.

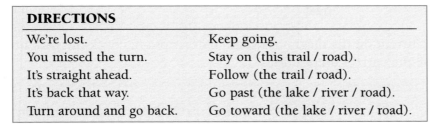

b **AUDIO** Try to complete the conversation above with expressions from the chart. Then listen and check your answers.

DIRECTIONS	
We're lost.	Keep going.
You missed the turn.	Stay on (this trail / road).
It's straight ahead.	Follow (the trail / road).
It's back that way.	Go past (the lake / river / road).
Turn around and go back.	Go toward (the lake / river / road).

c Work with a partner. Look at the map and ask for directions to different places. Use the expressions and make your own conversations.

★ = **You are here**

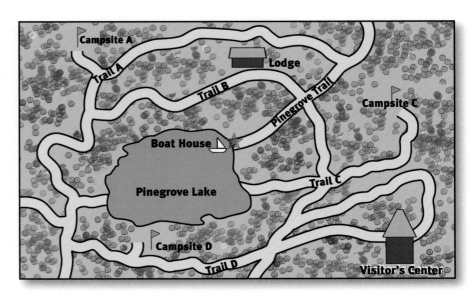

8 ▶ Listening

a Compare and discuss these animals. Which do you think are the most intelligent? The least?

bird   fish   chimpanzee   dolphin   horse   dog   cow   cat   elephant   whale

b **AUDIO** Listen to the conversation. Which animals are mentioned?

c **AUDIO** Listen again. Write T (true) or F (false).

1 A chimpanzee named Washoe used sign language to learn language. ___
2 Washoe learned about 35 words in total. ___
3 A parrot named Alex has learned to sing many different songs. ___
4 Research continues to focus mainly on animals learning language. ___
5 Zookeepers and veterinarians often have stories about animal intelligence. ___
6 Researchers are studying personal stories from pet owners. ___

d Have you heard about the research they discuss? Do you know of any similar research?

9 ▶ Writing

a Think of an experience you have had (or a story you have heard) which demonstrates a special characteristic of an animal (for example, intelligence, kindness, bravery). Write a paragraph about it.

> My friend, Roy, had a bird that was really intelligent. He taught the bird to say several words like, "Hello," "Goodbye," and "Thank you." The bird always said "Goodbye" when Roy left the house and "Hello" when he came home. The bird could also pick up small things and carry them.

b Read other students' paragraphs. What other animals and characteristics did they write about?

10 ▶ In Conversation

AUDIO What is Kenny going to do? Is Erica going to join him? Listen. Then read.

Erica: What's this? Are you going to volunteer at the zoo?

Kenny: I think so. I just talked to the supervisor there.

Erica: What did she say?

Kenny: She asked me to come to a volunteer training session. And she told me to think about which animals I'd like to work with.

Erica: Do you have to know a lot about animals?

Kenny: No. She told me not to worry about that.

Erica: When is the training session?

Kenny: Well, she wanted me to attend a session on Saturday, but I can't. There's one on Sunday, so I'm going to that one.

Erica: It sounds interesting. Maybe I'll do it, too.

Kenny: That would be fun!

11 ▶ Focus on Grammar

a Look at the chart. Fill in the blank and answer the question. Then find four more examples with *ask, tell,* and *want* in the conversation above.

1 *Asked / told / wanted* + object pronoun + _____ + verb
2 How do you make the negative form of a reported request with *want*?

Reported requests with *ask, tell,* and *want*		
"Please attend on Sunday."		"Don't arrive late."
She **asked** me		She **asked** me
She **told** him ▸ to attend on Sunday.		She **told** him ▸ not to arrive late.
She **wanted** us		She **didn't want** us ▸ to arrive late.

b **AUDIO** Listen to the volunteer training session. Use the prompts and try to report the supervisor's instructions in order.

take a name tag   begin   — touch the animals   check their names off the list
— feed the animals   take a ten-minute break

1 ask / them   *She asked them to check their names off the list.* _____
2 tell / them   _____
3 ask / Kenny   _____
4 tell / them   _____
5 want / them   _____
6 tell / them   _____

c **AUDIO** Compare answers. Then listen again and check your answers.

d Work with a partner. Take turns making requests. Then report your requests to another pair.

Example **A:** *Please lend me your pencil.*   **B:** *Ronald asked me to lend him a pencil.*

93

12 ▶ KnowHow: Choosing vocabulary to learn

a Different vocabulary is important or useful for different people. It depends on their needs. Look back at the vocabulary in this unit. Which words are likely to be useful for…

1 someone who lives in the mountains?
2 someone who lives near water?
3 someone who works with animals or loves animals?
4 a geologist?

b Choose five words from this unit that might be useful for you. Then compare your words. Explain why you chose them.

13 ▶ Speaking

a Work with a partner. Read situations 1–4. Then choose one of the animals below that you think would be good for each situation. Give reasons for your choices.

An adult cat named Midnight	Two goldfish	A small horse named Peppy
A large, gentle dog named Skip	A small dog named Otis	A kitten named Figgy
A very intelligent bird named Tweets (The bird can talk and pick up small objects.)		

1 The Fletchers are a family with three teenage children. They live out in the country and have a lot of space for a pet. The parents would like the children to take responsibility for the pet. The children want a pet they can have fun with. _____
2 The Kellys are a family with two young children. They live in an apartment in the city. They want their children to take responsibility for a pet. _____
3 Estelle is a woman in her 70s who is lonely. She would like a pet to keep her company, but she can't have a pet that needs a lot of care. _____
4 Samuel is a man in his 30s. He was injured in a car accident and has difficulty walking. He would like an animal for company, but also to help him. _____

b Compare and explain your choices to other students. How similar or different are they?

12 The right approach

✔ Office life and social customs
✔ Second conditional; indirect questions

1 ▶ Reading

a You're going to read an excerpt from a book of advice for people in the workplace. Look at the title and the picture. What kinds of topics do you think might be discussed?

AMERICA'S WORKPLACE COACH

Dear Jean

What They Don't Teach You at the Water Cooler

b Read the problems quickly. What advice do you think Jean will give?

c Turn the page around and read the advice. How similar were your thoughts?

PROBLEMS

1) The man at the desk next to me plays the radio all day. He has permission to do this. The problem is his choice of stations. I just can't stand the kind of music he plays. Do I have to get earplugs?

2) Recently I took one of my clients to lunch at a very nice restaurant. During our lunch, her cell phone rang three times. I realize that she has a very important position, but I found the calls very intrusive. What can I do about this in the future?

3) One of my co-workers comes into my cubicle and strains her neck trying to see whatever she can on my desk or calendar. I don't want to make a scene, but what should I do?

JEAN'S ADVICE

A) If he has permission to play his radio, I'm sure you can get permission to bring your own radio with headphones. Or maybe you could compromise and take turns. Ask him if you can pick the station sometimes. What's the worst that could happen? Try it!

B) Nothing! For whatever reason, she feels that she needs to be accessible to her office. I wouldn't take phone calls if I were in a restaurant with a colleague and neither would you. But she does and that's that. Granted, some people are not as considerate as they could be about cell phones, but they were invented to make life easier and they are here to stay.

C) Making a scene would probably not help the situation. But, you will have to take the initiative to stop this behavior. A direct approach would be to say something like, "I feel uncomfortable when you come in and look all over my desk." A less direct approach would be to just smile and say nicely, "Are you looking for something? Maybe I can help you find it," every time she comes in to take a look at your desk.

95

d Read the texts again. In situations 1–3 below, circle the response that agrees with the advice Jean gives. Explain your answers.

Situation 1:
a The person says nothing to the colleague and buys earplugs.
b The person talks to the colleague and asks to choose the radio station sometimes.

Situation 2:
a The person has dinner with the client and says nothing when the client answers her cell phone.
b The person goes to dinner with the client and says, "Please turn off your cell phone."

Situation 3:
a The next time the woman comes into the cubicle, the person says, "Are you looking for a pencil or something?"
b The person gets angry with the woman and tells her to stop doing it.

e Find a word or expression in the texts for each definition. (2) = problem 2; (A) = advice A.

1 disturbing you or your life (2) _____
2 show anger or strong feeling in public (3) _____
3 reach an agreement, with each side getting something they want (A) _____
4 possible to be reached or contacted (B) _____
5 careful not to upset people, thinking of others (B) _____
6 be the first to do something (C) _____

f What do you think of Jean's advice? How typical do you think these situations are?

2 Vocabulary: Expressions with *get, make,* and *take*

a Look at the diagrams. Look back at the texts in section 1 and find more expressions for each verb.

get	information, presents, _____, _____
make	a decision, a profit, _____, _____
take	someone to lunch, phone calls, _____, _____

b Choose one or two expressions from each diagram above. Write an example sentence for each one. Then compare sentences.

Example *make life easier—People say computers make life easier, but I'm not always sure.*

▼ Help Desk

You can use different verbs with *phone call.*

take a phone call = accept a call

get a phone call = receive a call

make a phone call = initiate a call

3 ▶ Focus on Grammar

a Look at the questions. Do they refer to <u>real</u> situations or <u>hypothetical or imaginary</u> situations?

b Look at the chart. What form of the verb is used in the…

    1 *if* clause?   2 main clause?

> What would you do in these situations? For example, would you tell your colleague to turn off the radio if it bothered you?

Second conditional

If *clause*	Main *clause*
If I **didn't like** the radio station,	I**'d ask** my co-worker to change stations.
If my co-worker **came** into my cubicle,	I**'d talk** to her.
If I **were** in a restaurant with a colleague,	I **wouldn't take** phone calls.

Note: *Were* is often used after *I, he, she,* and *it* in the second conditional especially in formal situations. *If I were you,....*

c Make sentences with the second conditional.

    1 If I <u>had</u> more experience, <u>I'd apply</u> for that job. (have / apply)

    2 He _____ along better with his co-workers if he _____ nicer. (get / be)

    3 What _____ you _____ if you _____ your job? (do / not like)

    4 We _____ more work done if we _____ so many breaks. (get / not take)

    5 If she _____ more money, she _____ happier with her job. (make / be)

    6 I _____ my job if it _____ boring. (not like / be)

    7 If they _____ work earlier, they _____ by 5:00. (start / finish)

d Make second conditional sentences about yourself. Use these ideas or your own.

    be the boss   have or get a different job   be happy   earn more money   like my job work in a big office   work alone   work long hours   have more time

    Examples *If I were the boss of my company, I'd have to work really long hours. I'd have more free time if I didn't commute to work.*

4 ▶ Listening

a AUDIO Listen. What are the problems mentioned?

b AUDIO Listen again. Make notes on the advice Alicia and Ryan give for each problem.

c Do you agree with the advice? Do you know any radio programs like this?

5 ▶ Vocabulary: Jobs and work

a Read the sentences. Put the underlined words in the correct diagrams below.

1 I'm supposed to <u>work nine to five</u>, but I always have to work <u>overtime,</u> too. It's a lot of hours.

2 Janine just started a new job. She was <u>hired</u> because she <u>has</u> a lot of <u>experience</u>. I think she'll <u>be promoted</u> quickly and get an even better position.

3 I wish I made more money. I need a <u>raise</u>! I should talk to my <u>boss</u>.

4 A: Chris is leaving the company.
   B: Oh, no! Was he <u>fired</u>?
   A: No, he <u>resigned</u>. He has another job.

I KNOW IT'S JUST MY FIRST DAY, BUT I BROUGHT THIS IN CASE I'M PROMOTED QUICKLY.

People	employer, employee, co-worker or colleague, client(s), _____

Hours & pay	to work part-time or full-time, salary, _____, _____, _____

Getting & keeping a job	to apply for a job, to have an interview, _____, _____, _____

Leaving a job	to be laid off, to retire, _____, _____

b Complete the paragraph with the correct form of a word or expression from the diagrams above.

Mr. Carter is my ¹____*boss*____; in fact, he owns the company. He is very nice to work for. All the ²_____ like him. I remember when I got the job. I had an ³_____ with him, and he asked me a lot of questions. I wasn't sure I had enough experience, but he ⁴_____ me. I started working ⁵_____, only about 20 hours a week, but now I work ⁶_____. Sometimes I work ⁷_____ on weekends, too. I don't mind the extra hours. I get a good ⁸_____, and I usually get a ⁹_____ every year.

6 ▶ Writing

a Write a note to another student. Ask for advice about a real or an imaginary problem.

> Dear Yoshi,
> Can you give me some advice? I have a problem with...

b Exchange notes with a partner. Write some advice for your partner's problem. Give the note back. Then work in groups. Read the different problems and advice. Does everyone agree with the advice?

7 Speaking

Work in groups. Use a marker and dice. Take turns and roll the dice. Move that number of spaces. Answer the question with the number you land on. Give reasons for your answers!

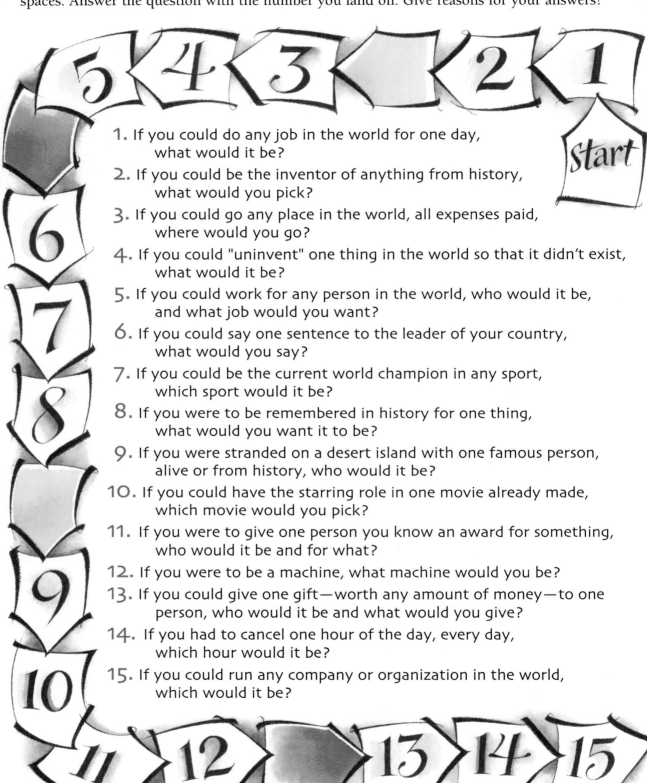

1. If you could do any job in the world for one day, what would it be?

2. If you could be the inventor of anything from history, what would you pick?

3. If you could go any place in the world, all expenses paid, where would you go?

4. If you could "uninvent" one thing in the world so that it didn't exist, what would it be?

5. If you could work for any person in the world, who would it be, and what job would you want?

6. If you could say one sentence to the leader of your country, what would you say?

7. If you could be the current world champion in any sport, which sport would it be?

8. If you were to be remembered in history for one thing, what would you want it to be?

9. If you were stranded on a desert island with one famous person, alive or from history, who would it be?

10. If you could have the starring role in one movie already made, which movie would you pick?

11. If you were to give one person you know an award for something, who would it be and for what?

12. If you were to be a machine, what machine would you be?

13. If you could give one gift—worth any amount of money—to one person, who would it be and what would you give?

14. If you had to cancel one hour of the day, every day, which hour would it be?

15. If you could run any company or organization in the world, which would it be?

8 Reading

a Write three pieces of advice you would give to a visitor about politeness and social customs in your country. Then compare your lists in groups. How much do you agree or disagree on?

Example   *In this country, it's typical to shake hands when you meet someone new.*

b Read the article quickly. Which story does each item relate to? Explain how it's related.

a coaster

a trash can

a bouquet of flowers

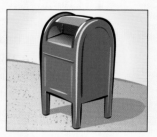
a mailbox

Social Customs & Cultural Misunderstandings: Your Experiences...

1

I was on my first trip to the United States. I was staying with friends with small children. We had a picnic in the park one day. We finished our picnic. I wanted to be helpful, so I picked up all our sandwich wrappers and put them into a large blue container that was nearby. When we were leaving the park I saw someone putting an envelope into the same blue container. Then I realized my mistake. I'd put our used sandwich wrappers into a mailbox.

- Contributed by Andreas Meyers

2

My husband and I were in France for work. We were invited to a French colleague's house for dinner, and we took some flowers for her. In my country, we always give an even number of flowers because an odd number is bad luck. So, we took a bouquet of twelve flowers. Unfortunately, in France the custom is to give an odd number of flowers. We felt terrible, but our colleague was very nice about it. We had an interesting conversation about politeness and customs in different places.

- Contributed by Chona Ling

3

During my first trip to Japan, I was taken to a local restaurant. I had been advised to try everything on my plate so as not to insult my Japanese hosts. They, in turn, were told to be patient with my American manners. Therefore they said nothing as I crunched my way through a tasteless wafer served with my meal. Later I realized we had all taken the advice too far: I had eaten a coaster.

- Contributed by Laura Pucher

c Read the article again. Work in small groups and discuss the questions.

1 When people do something wrong or inappropriate others often say, "Well, their intentions were good, but…." How could this apply to these situations?
2 Do you know any stories similar to these?
3 What other customs are there in your country related to these areas (for example, gift-giving, social occasions, eating)?

9 In Conversation

AUDIO What three things does Vincent ask about?
Listen. Then read.

Vincent: I'm going to a dinner party this evening. Do you have any idea what I should take as a gift?

Linda: Let's see…flowers or some chocolates would be nice.

Vincent: Great. Do you know what time I should arrive?

Linda: What do you mean?

Vincent: Well, the party is at 8:00. Is it typical to arrive right on time, or should I arrive a little later?

Linda: Oh, you should probably arrive on time.

Vincent: OK…Can you tell me where I can buy chocolates near here?

Linda: Yes, there's a shop near the train station.

Vincent: Oh, OK. Thanks for your help.

10 Focus on Grammar

a Use indirect questions to be polite or if you're not sure the person will know the answer. Compare direct and indirect questions in the chart and answer the questions.

1 What is the order of the subject and verb in indirect questions?
2 Is *if* used in *yes / no* questions or in *wh-* questions?
3 Do you use the auxiliary *do / did* in the *if* and *wh-* clauses?

Making indirect questions

Direct questions	Indirect questions
Where can I buy chocolates?	Can you tell me **where I can buy chocolates**?
What should I take as a gift?	Do you have any idea **what I should take as a gift**?
What time does the meeting start?	Could you tell me **what time the meeting starts**?
Did the meeting end at 5 o'clock?	Do you know **if the meeting ended at 5 o'clock**?

b Make indirect questions from the direct questions below. Use beginnings from the chart.

Example When does the flower shop open? *Do you know when the flower shop opens?*

1 Where is the conference room?
2 When does the post office close?
3 Where did your colleagues go?
4 Is there a nice restaurant near here?
5 Why did Maya leave work early?
6 What time does the party start?

c Work with a partner. Make conversations with indirect questions. Use these ideas or your own.

a classmate's name   the nearest bus stop   time class finishes   a café nearby   the time

Example A: *Can you tell me what that person's name is?*   B: *His name's Trent.*

KnowHow: Intonation patterns

a **AUDIO** Intonation is used to show enthusiasm, politeness, and other feelings. Listen to the two recordings of this conversation. Which one has a greater range of intonation and sounds more polite?

> A: Excuse me. Do you know where the conference room is?
> B: No, I'm afraid I don't. Try asking at the front desk.

Now practice the conversation that has a greater range of intonation.

b **AUDIO** Listen and practice the conversation below. Try to use the intonation you hear.

> A: Can you tell me if there's a nice restaurant near here?
> B: Yes, there's an Italian restaurant on the next block.
> A: OK. Thank you.

Language in Action: Politeness

a **AUDIO** Listen. Number the conversations in the order you hear them.

A___   B___   C___

b **AUDIO** Listen again. Write the number of the conversation(s) in which you hear each expression.

BEING POLITE	
_1_ Let me give you my card.	___ We'd like you to have this.
___ Here's my card.	___ How nice!
___ Please contact me any time.	___ It's my pleasure.
___ Thank you.	___ I'll be in touch.
___ Would you be able to…	___ It was nice to meet you.
___ I'd really appreciate it if…	___ Have a good trip (back).
___ I'll see what I can do.	___ Goodbye.

c Work with a partner. Use the expressions and practice your own conversations for the three situations. Remember to use a good range of intonation!

1 exchanging business cards and saying goodbye
2 asking someone to do something politely
3 presenting a small gift and saying thank you

Grammar

1 Read the text. What can you do to protect yourself from lightning?

BELIEFS ABOUT LIGHTNING
Lightning has been the subject of superstition for centuries. For example, many people believe that if you are struck by lightning, you will die. In fact, 97 percent of those struck live. There is a more recent belief that if you play golf, you are more likely to be a victim. Not so. Most lightning injuries are work-related, including injuries to construction and utility workers.
Should you wear rubber-soled shoes or a rubber raincoat for protection? If you wore these during a lightning storm, it wouldn't matter. You *should* avoid being the tallest object in an area, though, and you should stay away from trees. If you can get to a building, you'll be even safer.

2 Fill in the blanks with the correct form of the verbs. Use the first conditional.

1 If lightning *strikes* you, you probably *won't die*. (strike / not die)
2 You _____ safe if you _____ inside. (be / go)
3 You _____ at risk if you _____ the tallest object in an area. (be / be)

3 Complete the conversation with appropriate advice modals.

Alina: I'm planning to go hiking in the woods, but I'm afraid I might get lost. What ¹ *should* I do?

Pedro: Well, to start with, you ² _____ to take a map of the area.
Alina: ³ _____ I take a compass, too?
Pedro: Definitely. And you ⁴ _____ to tell someone where you are going and when you'll be back.
Alina: I was planning to go alone. I guess I ⁵ _____ do that, should I?
Pedro: No, you ⁶ _____ to go hiking by yourself. You'd ⁷ _____ find someone to go with you.
Alina: Would you like to come? You seem to know a lot about hiking!

4 Rewrite the sentences. Use reported requests.

1 "Give me your notes from the meeting," Sid said to Mary.
Sid told *Mary to give him the notes from the meeting.*
2 "Could you attend the meeting for me?" I asked them.
I asked _____.
3 "Please greet the visitor," he said to me.
He wanted _____.
4 "Call me right away!" she said to me.
She told _____.

5 Fill in the blanks with the correct forms of the verbs in parentheses. Use the second conditional.

Carl has been asking for advice about improving his employment situation. Here are some samples:

1 If you _____ (have) more experience, you would probably get a promotion.
2 If you worked overtime, you _____ (make) some extra money.
3 You would get a better position if you _____ (take) a management course.
4 You _____ (make) a better impression on clients if you wore a suit every day.

6 ▶ Rewrite the direct questions as indirect questions.

1 Where is the meeting?
Do you know *where the meeting is?*
2 Does everybody know about the meeting? Could you tell me _____?
3 Who is the main speaker?
Do you know _____?
4 What are they going to discuss?
Can you tell me _____?
5 What did they talk about at the last meeting?
Do you know _____?

Vocabulary

7 ▶ Complete the sentences with the expressions below. One expression is used twice.

coast   take over   make   pull over
take on   get   raise

1 Did you know that PTCorp is planning to _____ our company?
2 Can you _____ a decision now or would you like to think about it?
3 Their house on the _____ has beautiful views of the ocean.
4 We _____ a lot of phone calls in the morning, but in the afternoon the phone hardly rings.
5 Are you ready to _____ such a big job? It's going to be very difficult.
6 I hope I get a _____ pretty soon. I really need more money.
7 We got a flat tire so we had to _____ to the side of the road and fix it.

Fun Spot

Change one letter in each word so that the new word matches the definition.

Fire _*Hire*_ = to give someone a job

8 ▶ The underlined verbs in the sentences below are incorrect. Correct them.

1 You'd better <u>carry</u> some nice clothes for your job interview.
2 Can you <u>take</u> that magazine with you when you come over? I want to read it.
3 We left the house late so we <u>lost</u> the bus and had to take a taxi.
4 Did you <u>know</u> Indira at that party or were you introduced later?
5 I'm tired of <u>looking at</u> TV! Can we play a game or something?

Recycling Center 🔄

9 ▶ Fill in the blanks with *make* or *do* in the correct form.

1 It's never easy to _*make*_ a living as a farmer.
2 I'm good at _____ housework but Dana is much better at _____ the meals.
3 Can you _____ me a favor? I need someone to _____ the shopping for me. I've already _____ a list of everything I need.
4 It's not easy for me to _____ a decision about this. I don't want to _____ a mistake!
5 I've been _____ business with them for 20 years, and I've always _____ a profit from our deals.

Design _____ = to leave your job or position
Employer _____ = a person who works for somebody
Toast _____ = the area of land that is next to or close to the ocean
Rider _____ = a large, natural stream of water
Hose _____ = a person who receives a guest

Keep on talking!

1 ▶ Personal bingo

1 Work with a partner. Fill in the empty squares on the bingo card. Write activities similar to the ones that are there. Leave blanks for people to sign their names on the card.

2 Walk around the class. Ask different people questions about the items on your card. If someone says, "Yes," ask the person to sign the card. The first person to get five signatures in a row—across, down, or diagonally—"wins" the game.

Example   *Did you wash the dishes last night?*

PERSONAL BINGO

		(Name)_____ had a good time last weekend	
	washed the dishes last night			
		often unwinds by walking in the park		
likes to iron				would like to go scuba diving
	had a hard day yesterday			

2 ▶ What do you know about language?

Work with a partner. Try to answer these questions. When you finish, compare answers with another pair.

Language Quiz

1 How many languages are there in the world?
   a 27,000   b 2,700   c 270,000   d 7,000

2 Which language do linguists consider the most difficult?
   a Basque   b Chinese   c English   d Russian

3 What language do all airline pilots need to speak?
   a French   b Spanish   c English   d German

4 The word *tycoon* means a wealthy businessperson. What language does it come from?
   a Dutch   b Norwegian   c Japanese   d Spanish

5 Which of the following letters is **not** among the five most common consonants in English?
   a L   b R   c N   d C

6 What does *gobbledygook* mean?
   a someone who eats too fast   b meaningless language   c bad tasting food

7 The word *buckaroo* is a slang term for cowboy. What language does it come from?
   a Dutch   b Norwegian   c Japanese   d Spanish

(For answers to the quiz, go to page 111.)

UNIT

3 ▶ Been there, done that

Sports	Volleyball		
Restaurants			
Vacation places			
English books or magazines			
Songs in English	"Blue Skies" (Song Title)		
People			

1   Work with a partner. Look at the list of categories in the chart. Fill in the chart with the names of three specific items for each category.

2   Walk around the class and talk to different people. Try to find people who have done (or *visited, been to, played, read, seen, heard…*) these things. Take notes.

Example questions: *Have you ever played volleyball? Have you eaten at Tom's Restaurant?*

3   Compare your notes with the class. What things have most people done or not done?

UNIT

4 ▶ Locked out! Student A

(For B's part of this activity, go to page 109.)

1   Read these six sentences from a story. Your partner has seven sentences from the same story. The sentences are not in logical order.

- On three, Sheila swung from his living room window to her bedroom window, which was only about ten feet away.

- She asked her next door neighbor Doug to help her, so Doug went to find a locksmith.

- He said, "All of the locksmiths are closed, but I have an idea! We'll use this rope."

- Doug was standing on the roof of the building, holding one end of the rope.

- Suddenly, the wind blew her bedroom door shut.

- While she was swinging in the air, Doug said, "Don't look down!"

2   Work with your partner. Read your sentences. Listen to your partner's sentences. Put the sentences in logical order.

Here is the first sentence:

1   Sheila had the scariest experience of her life last year....

5 ▶ The world of advertising

1 Work in small groups. Look at the photo. What kind of advertisement do you think the photo could be used in? What product(s) might it advertise?

2 Think of a product that you would like to advertise. Discuss questions like these with the group.

> **What's the best medium for your advertisement? (Newspapers, television...)**
> **Who do you want to buy your product or service?**

3 Work together to write an advertisement for the product or service without saying what it is. Include details about what it does, what it is made of, etc.

4 Present your advertisement to the class. They will ask questions and try to guess what it is.

6 ▶ What's important!

	Scientist	Politician	Musician	Teacher	Accountant
honest					
outgoing					
eccentric					
ambitious					
creative					
stubborn					
enthusiastic					
shy					
intelligent					
generous					

1 Work with a partner. Look at the chart and check the three personality characteristics that you think are most important in each profession.

2 Work with another pair and compare your charts. Discuss the reasons for your answers. Which characteristics do you agree on? Which do you disagree on?

UNIT 7 ▶ Entrepreneurs

1 Work in small groups. Choose one group as the "Investors." The other group(s) are the "Entrepreneurs." Follow the instructions below for each type.

Entrepreneurs: There is a group of investors in your community interested in investing in small businesses. Create a proposal for a business that could be successful in your community. As you work, consider questions like these:

What kind of business would you like to start? (A store, making a product to sell...?)
Who would your customers be?
Why do think the business would be successful?
What would you need to start?

Investors: You are a group of businesspeople interested in investing in new businesses in this community. Make a list of as many different kinds of businesses as possible that you think might be successful.

2 **Entrepreneurs**, present your ideas to the Investors. **Investors**, select the idea(s) you think would be most successful and explain why.

UNIT 8 ▶ A communication crossword: Student A

(For B's part of this activity, go to page 111.)

1 Work with a partner. A, you have the *across* words in this crossword puzzle. Your partner has the *down* words. Help your partner guess the across words. Don't say the words. Give clues.

Example of clue: *Number 5 across is the opposite of young.* (Answer: OLD)

2 Change roles. Listen to B's clues for the *down* words. Complete your puzzle.

3 Check your answers with B.

4 Locked out! Student B

(For A's part of this activity, go to page 106.)

1 Read these seven sentences from a story. Your partner has six sentences from the same story. The sentences are not in logical order.

> • She didn't, and believe it or not, she made it safely into her bedroom.
>
> • But when Doug came back, he was holding a long rope in his hand.
>
> • One warm but windy morning, Sheila was reading a book in the living room of her apartment on the third floor of a small apartment building.
>
> • Ten minutes later, Sheila was standing in the window of Doug's living room.
>
> • The other end of the rope was tied around Sheila's body, just under her arms.
>
> • Doug counted to three.
>
> • Sheila tried to open the door, but it was locked and she didn't have the key.

2 Work with your partner. Read your sentences. Listen to your partner's sentences. Put the sentences in logical order.

Here is the first sentence:

1 Sheila had the scariest experience of her life last year....

9 Thirty years ago

1 Think about how your community has changed in the last 20 or 30 years. Make a list of the differences between then and now.

2 Work with a partner and discuss the changes you have written down. Decide which changes are positive and which are negative.

3 Report to the class and compare your lists. What similarities are there in all the lists? Does everyone agree about which changes are positive and which are negative?

UNIT
10 ▶ Tried and true? Pair A

(For Pair B's part of this activity, go to page 111.)

1 Work with a partner. Look at the expressions below. Prepare a presentation of each expression. Use these questions to help you:

What do you think the expression means?
Is it true or does it offer good advice?
Can you give a concrete example or story from your own experience that supports the expression?

Don't judge a book by its cover.

Look before you leap.

Too many cooks spoil the broth.

2 Present your expressions to **Pair B**.
Then listen to **Pair B**'s presentations.

UNIT
11 ▶ Where could this be? Student A

(For B's part of this activity, go to page 112.)

1 Look at the small photograph on this page and the information under it. Your partner, **B**, has a large version of this picture, but no information about it. Ask **B** to speculate about the picture. Ask questions like these:

Where do you think this might be?
What could the white area in the picture be?
Do you think the weather in this place is cold or hot?

2 Now answer your partner's questions about the large picture on this page. Use your imagination. Speculate about what the picture might be.

3 After you and your partner have discussed both pictures, tell each other about the pictures, using the information on your page.

Uyuni, Bolivia
The world's largest salt flat
9,000 square km

UNIT 8 ▶ A communication crossword: Student B

(For A's part of this activity, go to page 108.)

1 Work with a partner. B, you have the *down* words in this crossword puzzle. Your partner has the *across* words. Help your partner guess the down words. Don't say the words. Give clues.

> Example of clue: *Number 1 down is a popular seasoning. It is white.* (Answer: SALT)

2 Change roles. Listen to A's clues for the *down* words. Complete your puzzle.

3 Check your answers with A.

ACROSS ⟶

DOWN ↓

	¹S			²C				³B
	A			H			⁴G	A
⁵	L			O		⁶F	O	K
	T			⁷P		E	L	E
⁸C						⁹A	D	
O			¹⁰G			T		
¹¹O			R			H		¹²I
K			I			E		C
			L		¹³	R		E
¹⁴			L			S		D

UNIT 10 ▶ Tried and true? Pair B

(For Pair A's part of this activity, go to page 110.)

1 Work with a partner. Look at the expressions below. Prepare a presentation of each expression. Use these questions to help you:

What do you think the expression means?
Is it true or does it offer good advice?
Can you give a concrete example or a story from your own experience that supports the expression?

> *Don't put all your eggs in one basket.*
>
> *Don't count your chickens before they are hatched.*
>
> *Many hands make light work.*

2 Present you expressions to **Pair A**. Then listen to **Pair A's** presentations.

(Language Quiz Answers: 1b, 2a, 3c, 4c, 5d, 6b, 7d)

UNIT 11 ▶ Where could this be? Student B

(For A's part of this activity, go to page 110.)

1 Look at the small photograph on this page and the information under it. Your partner, **A**, has a large version of this picture, but no information about it. Ask **A** to speculate about the picture. Ask questions like these:

Where do you think this might be? What are the objects next to the sea in the picture? Do you think they might be man-made?

Giants' Causeway, Northern Ireland
A rock formation
The result of volcanic action 60 million years ago

2 Now answer your partner's questions about the large picture on this page. Use your imagination. Speculate about what the picture might be.

3 After you and your partner have discussed both pictures, tell each other about the pictures, using the information on the page.

UNIT 12 ▶ Role play: I'm so sorry...

1 Work with a partner. Create a role-play based on the following situation.

A: You're at your new boss's house for a small party. You don't know anyone well. You trip over something and accidentally break a small vase sitting on a table. You feel terrible. Apologize, offer to replace the vase, etc.

B: You're having a small party for some employees. A new employee (who you know is really nervous) accidentally breaks a small vase of yours. You know he / she feels terrible. In fact, the vase was a present that you never really liked. Accept the apology and assure the employee that it isn't really a problem.

2 Now work with a new partner. Do the role-play again. Does the role-play change?

Vocabulary Reference

This section brings together key words and expressions from each unit. Use *Word for Word* to note down other important words that you want to remember.

Unit 1: All work and no play

band (*n.*)
bill (*n.*)
cartoon (*n.*)
chore (*n.*)
conference (*n.*)
darkness (*n.*)
dislike (*v.*)
excuse (*n.*)
exercise (*v.*)
foreign (*adj.*)
funny (*adj.*)
garbage (*n.*)

hate (*v.*)
helpful (*adj.*)
honestly (*adv.*)
improve (*v.*)
iron (*v.*)
laundry (*n.*)
leisure (*n.*)
loft (*n.*)
meteorologist (*n.*)
mop (*v.*)
neither (*conj.*)
nonstop (*adj.*)

observation (*n.*)
old-time (*adj.*)
shift (*n.*)
socialize (*v.*)
summarize (*v.*)
sunlight (*n.*)
sweep (*v.*)
unwind (*v.*)
vacuum (*v.*)
volleybag (*n.*)
volunteer (*v.*)
wide (*adj.*)

Expressions
be by yourself
forget your worries
get away
get together
take it easy

Unit 2: Making sense

achieve (-ment) (*v., n.*)
artistically (*adv.*)
aspect (*n.*)
bake (*v.*)
beyond (*prep.*)
clash (*n.*)
compose (*v.*)
creative (-ity) (*adj., n.*)
curious (-sity) (*adj., n.*)
curtain (*n.*)
destroy (*v.*)
educate (-tion) (*v., n.*)
embarrassing (*adj.*)
evolve (*v.*)
excite (-ment) (*v., n.*)
expert (*n.*)
explore (-ation) (*v., n.*)
fabulous (*adj.*)
flabbergasted (*adj.*)
gifted (*adj.*)

govern (*v.*)
hectic (*adj.*)
highlight (*n.*)
intelligence (*n.*)
lead (*v.*)
lilac (*adj.*)
linguistics (*n.*)
manage (*v.*)
math (mathematics) (*n.*)
neuroscientist (*n.*)
normally (*adv.*)
novelist (*n.*)
old-fashioned (*adj.*)
orderly (*adj.*)
original (*adj.*)
oven (*n.*)
phenomenon (*n.*)
pickle (*n.*)
playful (*adj.*)

possible (-ility) (*adj., n.*)
produce (*v.*)
rectangle (*n.*)
rule (*n.*)
sensation (*n.*)
sense (*n.*)
shape (*n.*)
shorthand (*n.*)
sight (*n.*)
similar (-ity) (*adj., n.*)
sleepy (*adj.*)
smell (*v., n.*)
soft (*adj.*)
strength (*n.*)
stupid (-ity) (*adj., n.*)
symptom (*n.*)
synesthesia (*n.*)
translate (-tion) (*v., n.*)
velvet (*adj.*)

Expressions
hold on
out loud
run in (families)
text messaging

Unit 3: Big screen, small screen

acting (n.)
animated (adj.)
arithmetic (n.)
attraction (n.)
casting (adj., n.)
cause (v.)
character (n.)
classic (n.)
clue (n.)
comedy (n.)
confused (-ing) (adj.)
costume (n.)
cowboy (n.)
criminal (n.)
criticism (n.)
direct (-ing) (v., n)
disappointed (-ing)
 (adj.)
documentary (n.)
drawing (n.)
entire (adj.)

evidence (n.)
exceptional (adj.)
excited (-ing) (adj.)
extra (n.)
fact (n.)
fair (adj.)
fascinated (-ing) (adj.)
fiction (n.)
frustrated (-ing) (adj.)
galaxy (n.)
genuine (adj.)
ghost (n.)
horror (adj.)
improvement (n.)
involve (v.)
irony (n.)
killer (n.)
laundry (n.)
literacy (n.)
lowered (adj.)
mood (n.)

murderer (n.)
obligation (n.)
participant (n.)
passive (-ivity) (adj., n.)
pleasure (n.)
plot (n.)
poll (n.)
producer (n.)
psychology (adj., n.)
queen (n.)
quit (v.)
rapidly (adv.)
rating (n.)
responsible (adj.)
review (-er) (n.)
rewarding (adj.)
satisfaction (n.)
science (n.)
screenplay (n.)
shoot (v.)
solve (v.)

species (n.)
steadily (adv.)
superb (adj.)
suppose (v.)
tense (adj.)
theory (n.)
tiring (adj.)
trap (v.)
universe (n.)
unknown (adj.)
unrealistic (adj.)
violent (-ence) (adj., n.)
western (n., adj.)

Unit 4: In the mind's eye

absent-minded (adj.)
accurate (adj.)
brand-new (adj.)
childhood (adj., n.)
come back (v.)
come in (v.)
come over (v.)
dreamy (adj.)
errand (n.)
familiar (adj.)
flash (n.)
get hurt (v.)
go away (v.)
go on (v.)
go over (v.)
hill (n.)
joy (n.)
left-handed (adj.)
memorize (v.)
painting (n.)
pleasant (adj.)

remind (v.)
right-handed (adj.)
river (n.)
self-taught (adj.)
static (adj.)
surprisingly (adv.)
unable (adj.)
urgency (n.)
well-dressed (adj.)

Expressions
It's on the tip of my
 tongue.
It'll come to me.

Word for Word

Unit 5: Stuff of life

associate (n.)
autograph (v.)
basket (n.)
bother (v.)
broken (adj.)
button (n.)
can opener (n.)
close (v.)
clothes hanger (n.)
coin (n.)
contradiction (n.)
contribute (v.)
corporation (n.)
cotton (adj., n.)
dial (n.)
diamond (adj., n.)
dry (adj.)
dust (v., n.)
essence (n.)
estimate (v.)
gadget (n.)

gesture (n.)
gold (adj., n.)
grid (n.)
hammer (n.)
hair dryer (n.)
handle (n.)
hole (n.)
household (adj., n.)
humor (n.)
indoors (adv.)
irritate (v.)
itch (n.)
knife (n.)
leather (adj., n.)
locate (v.)
materialism (n.)
microwave (oven) (n.)
mime (n.)
necklace (n.)
press (v.)
put away (v.)

put down (v.)
put on (v.)
remove (v.)
repair (v., n.)
scissors (n.)
scratch (v.)
screw (n.)
screwdriver (n.)
sentimental (adj.)
shelf (n.)
silver (adj., n.)
slipper (n.)
sole (adj.)
solve (v.)
stereo (n.)
take off (v.)
toaster oven (n.)
tool (n.)
turn down (v.)
turn up (v.)
unlikely (adj.)

unseen (adj.)
weathered (adj.)
wet (adj.)
wooden (adj.)
worn (adj.)

Word for Word

Unit 6: Interesting characters

agreeable (adj.)
ambitious (adj.)
analysis (n.)
basket-weaving (n.)
behave (-ior) (v., n.)
complicated (adj.)
conclude (v.)
conform (v.)
convinced (adj.)
dawn (n.)
discover (v.)
dusk (n.)
eccentric (-ity) (adj., n.)
efficiently (adv.)
embrace (v.)
enthusiastic (adj.)
graphology (n.)
idealistic (adj.)
immune system
insane (adj.)
loop (n.)

mildly (adv.)
nonconforming (adj.)
obsessed (adj.)
outlandish (adj.)
participate (v.)
phrenology (n.)
self-image (n.)
shared (adj.)
shave (v.)
show up (v.)
sky-diving (n.)
slant (n.)
stroke (n.)
stubborn (adj.)
trait (n.)
unconventional (adj.)
unfriendly (adj.)
unpopular (adj.)
vote (v.)

Expressions
as opposed to
out of step

Word for Word

Unit 7: Trade and treasure

accumulate (v.)
afford (v.)
air conditioner (n.)
annual (adj.)
appointment (n.)
babysit (v.)
barter (v.)
borrow (v.)
bundle (n.)
clearly (adv.)
clever (adj.)
contribution (n.)
deal (n.)
demonstrate (v.)
donation (n.)
earn (v.)
file (n.)
financial (adj.)
flashlight (n.)
fool (n.)
frugally (adv.)

generation (n.)
generous (-sity)
  (adj., n.)
goods (n.)
honor (v.)
housework (n.)
identification (n.)
increase (v.)
inflation (n.)
initially (adv.)
inspire (v.)
lend (v.)
modest (adj.)
owe (v.)
pay back (v.)
penny (n.)
president (n.)
proceeds (n.)
profit (n.)
quiet-spoken (adj.)
rise (n.)

ruin (n.)
save (v.)
services (n.)
snack (n.)
trade (n., v.)
treasure hunt (n.)
treat (n.)
trophy (n.)
underneath (prep.)
waste (v.)
winnings (n.)

Expressions
higher learning
take a look at
  (something)

Word for Word

Unit 8: A taste of it

agriculture (-al) (adj.,
  n.)
bad-tempered (adj.)
barbeque (v.)
beauty (n.)
beverage (n.)
boil (v.)
camel (n.)
carbonated (adj.)
chop (v.)
cinnamon (n.)
commercially (adv.)
consume (v.)
craze (n.)
craziness (n.)
crisp (adj.)
demand (n.)
desert (n.)
digest (-ion) (v., n.)
economics (n.)
economy (n.)

elaborate (adj.)
fair (n.)
farm (-ed) (n., adj.)
farmer (n.)
feather (n.)
fork (n.)
fry (v.)
funny-looking (adj.)
gas (n.)
grape (n.)
grapefruit (n.)
grill (n., v.)
hate (n., v.)
honesty (n.)
iced tea (n.)
inch (n.)
industry (n.)
king (n.)
lemonade (n.)
mania (n.)
mansion (n.)

mayonnaise (n.)
mix (-ture) (v., n.)
oil (n.)
ostrich (n.)
palace (n.)
peak (adj., n.)
peel (v.)
potato chip (n.)
prince (n.)
quality control (n.)
reaction (n.)
rock (n.)
scientific (adj.)
shampoo (n.)
show off (v.)
slice (v., n.)
sparrow (n.)
steam (v.)
sugar (n.)
swallow (v.)
teaspoon (n.)

throat (n.)
tower (n.)
value (-able) (n., adj.)
variety (n.)
war (n.)
wealth (n.)
weigh (v.)
wool (n.)

Word for Word

Unit 9: By land and by sea

accommodation (*n.*)
against (*prep.*)
aisle seat (*n.*)
announcement (*n.*)
anxious (*adj.*)
boat-builder (*n.*)
cabin (*n.*)
captain (*n.*)
carry-on bag (*n.*)
chance (*n.*)
charge (*n.*)
check in (*v.*)
check out (*v.*)
conductor (*n.*)
counter (*n.*)
crew (*n.*)
emergency (*n.*)
expedition (*n.*)
expertise (*n.*)
exploration (*n.*)
explorer (*n.*)

fluent (-cy) (*adj., n.*)
greet (*v.*)
gypsy (*n.*)
hand luggage (*n.*)
hang (*v.*)
harness (*n.*)
highway (*n.*)
insist (*v.*)
join (*v.*)
journey (*n.*)
land (*v.*)
lobby (*n.*)
mast (*n.*)
mess (*n.*)
muffled (*adj.*)
murmur (*v.*)
obstacle (*n.*)
one-way (*adj.*)
pack (*v.*)
passport (*n.*)
pillow (*n.*)

poet (*n.*)
purely (*adv.*)
reception desk (*n.*)
recommend (*v.*)
reed (*n.*)
reservation (*n.*)
roar (*n.*)
rope (*n.*)
round-trip (*adj.*)
sail (-ing) (*n., adj.*)
sleepy (*adj.*)
smoothly (*adv.*)
soak (*v.*)
stolen (*adj.*)
take off (*v.*)
torrential (*adj.*)
traveler's check
   (*n.*)
visa (*n.*)
voyage (*n.*)
waterline (*n.*)

window seat (*n.*)

Expressions
   fill out (a form)
   go sightseeing
   make sense

Unit 10: Hard to believe?

aggressive (*adj.*)
assumption (*n.*)
belief (*n.*)
bottom (*n.*)
bowling (*n.*)
bury (-ied) (*v., adj.*)
cleaner (*n.*)
clerk (*n.*)
competition (*n.*)
courtroom (*n.*)
cure (*v.*)
doubt (*n.*)
drop (*v.*)
face (-ial) (*n., adj.*)
fever (*n.*)
gang (*n.*)
genuine (*adj.*)
get injured (*v.*)
gum (*n.*)
ice hockey (*n.*)
judge (*v.*)

lose (*v.*)
luck (-y) (*n., adj.*)
lucky charm (*n.*)
old-time (*adj.*)
ought (*v.*)
pan (*n.*)
protective (*adj.*)
race (*n.*)
rodeo riding (*n.*)
soul (*n.*)
spill (*v.*)
stranger (*n.*)
superstition (*n.*)
tap (*v.*)
team (*n.*)
tennis court (*n.*)
tire (*n.*)
toward (*prep.*)
uniform (*n.*)
warning (*n.*)
wipe (*v.*)

Expressions
   be supposed to
   make a good
      impression
   rhythm and blues
   rock and roll

Unit 11: Down to earth

attend (v.)
bathtub toy (n.)
beachcomber (n.)
benefit (n.)
bravery (n.)
calm (adj.)
chimpanzee (n.)
coast (n.)
contact (v.)
converge (v.)
cow (n.)
current (n.)
desert (n.)
dolphin (n.)
feed (v.)
forest (n.)
gardening (n.)
gentle (adj.)
geologist (n.)
glove (n.)
goldfish (n.)

island (n.)
health (-y) (n., adj.)
high-tech (adj.)
hill (n.)
junk (n.)
kindness (n.)
kitten (n.)
lake (n.)
landscape (n.)
lonely (adj.)
mountain (range) (n.)
name tag (n.)
natural (adj.)
northwestern (adj.)
oceanographer (n.)
pattern (n.)
plastic (adj., n.)
publish (v.)
rainforest (n.)
random (adj.)
refine (v.)

research (-er) (n.)
river (n.)
satellite (n.)
sea (n.)
session (n.)
ship (-ment) (v., n.)
shore (n.)
sign language (n.)
swap meet (n.)
track (v.)
trail (n.)
valley (n.)
veterinarian (n.)
wash up (v.)
waterfall (n.)
whale (n.)
zoo / zookeeper
   (n.)

Word for Word

Unit 12: The right approach

accessible (adj.)
anger (-ry) (n., adj.)
approach (n.)
bouquet (n.)
champion (n.)
coaster (n.)
compromise (v.)
conference room (n.)
considerate (adj.)
container (n.)
co-worker (n.)
crunch (v.)
cubicle (n.)
custom (n.)
disturb (v.)
earplugs (n.)
even (adj.)
expense (n.)
fire / be fired (v.)
granted (adv.)
headphones (n.)

hire / be hired (v.)
host (n.)
imaginary (adj.)
initiate (v.)
intrusive (adj.)
lay off / be laid off (v.)
leader (n.)
mailbox (n.)
manners (n.)
misunderstanding (n.)
neck (n.)
odd (adj.)
overtime (n.)
picnic (n.)
plate (n.)
polite (-ness) (adj., n)
promote (v.)
raise (n.)
resign (v.)
retire (v.)
salary (n.)

sandwich wrapper (n.)
strain (v.)
stranded (adj.)
take turns (v.)
tasteless (adj.)
trash can (n.)
upset (v.)
wafer (n.)

Expressions
be in touch
make a scene
take the initiative

Word for Word

Grammar Reference

This section reviews and expands the main grammar points presented in this book.

Review of questions and short answers: Present and past	Unit 1
Question	**Response**
Present continuous Are you living here now?	Yes, I am. / No, I'm not.
Simple Present Do you enjoy walking in the park? Does he like to go for walks?	Yes, I do. / No, I don't. Yes, he does. / No, he doesn't.
Simple past Did you go out last night?	Yes, I did. / No, I didn't.
Present perfect Have you done your chores?	Yes, I have. / No, I haven't.

Do / Does / Did can be both an auxiliary and a main verb: *Did you do your homework?*

Responding with *so / neither* and *too / either* (review)			Unit 1
Statement	**so / neither**	**too / either (review)**	**Disagreeing**
I am relaxing today. I'm not working today.	So am I. Neither am I.	I am too. I'm not either.	I'm not. I am.
I enjoy walking. He doesn't like jogging.	So do I. Neither does she.	I do too. She doesn't either.	I don't. She does.
We did chores yesterday. I didn't watch TV last night.	So did we. Neither did I.	We did too. I didn't either.	We didn't. I did.
I've ironed my shirts. Roy hasn't washed the car.	So have I. Neither has Sam.	I have too. Sam hasn't either.	I haven't. Sam has.

So / neither and *too / either* (usually in informal situations) are used to give short responses.

Gerunds and infinitives	Unit 1
Verb + gerund (verb + -ing)	
They **enjoy cooking.**	He **can't stand ironing.**
Verb + infinitive (to + base form)	
I **hope to finish** the chores by 10 a.m.	We**'re planning to go** away next weekend.
Verb + gerund OR infinitive	
We **like listening** to music. OR We **like to listen** to music. Arturo **loves playing** chess. OR Arturo **loves to play** chess.	

Common verbs followed by a gerund: *enjoy, can't stand, don't mind.*
Common verbs followed by an infinitive (base form) with *to: hope, plan, need, would like, want.*
Common verbs followed by either the gerund or infinitive: *like, love, hate.*

Present continuous	Unit 2
Subject + be	**Verb + -ing**
I'm (not) You're (aren't) He's / She's (isn't) We're / They're (aren't)	studying English.
Questions	**Answers**
Are you studying? Is he studying? What are they studying?	Yes, I am. / No, I'm not. Yes, he is. / No, he isn't. French.

The present continuous is used for:
1. Actions happening right now:
My cell phone is ringing, but I can't find it.
2. Actions happening around now
(they might not be happening at this moment):
I'm working a lot of hours this week.

3. Changing or developing situations:
New words are always coming into the language.
4. Arrangements and plans in the future, usually when time and place are decided:
They're starting their vacation on Sunday.

Common categories of stative (non-action) verbs	Unit 2
Descriptions and the senses	
be, look, seem, sound, see, hear, taste, smell	The flowers smell wonderful. Jeremy looks tired.
Possessions	
have, own	I don't own a car, but I have a bicycle.
Emotions and attitudes	
like, love, hate, want, need	Dina loves classical music. The children like sports.
Ideas	
think, understand, know, believe	I don't understand the question. She knows a lot about synesthesia.

Stative (or non-action) verbs express a state or condition, not an activity. They are not usually used in the continuous tenses: *I like sports* NOT ~~*I'm liking sports.*~~
Some verbs have both stative and action meanings. They can take the continuous form if they are describing an action: *look, feel, taste, smell, have,* and *think.*
Stative: *The soup tastes delicious.*   Action: *I'm tasting the soup to see if it needs more salt.*

Present perfect simple		Unit 3
Statements		
Subject	**have (has)**	**Past participle**
I / You / We / They He / She / It	have / haven't has / hasn't	seen the movie.
Questions		**Answers**
Have you seen it? Has she seen it? How many movies has she made? What have they done?		Yes, I have. / No, I haven't. Yes, she has. / No, she hasn't. Two. They've written the script.

Present perfect simple + *still / yet / already*	Unit 3

We **still** haven't seen that new movie.
Terry hasn't acted in a movie **yet**.
Have you seen that new documentary **yet?**
They've **already** seen that movie.
They've seen that movie **already**.

Already is used when something has happened sooner than expected. *Still* and *yet* are used when something is expected but hasn't happened.
Still usually goes before *have / has* in a sentence. *Yet* usually goes at the end of the sentence. *Already* can go after the auxiliary or at the end of the sentence.

Expressions of obligation and permission — Unit 3

	Present	Past
Obligation	You **need / don't need to** work today. You **have / don't have to** work today. You **must / must not** leave early.	You **needed / didn't need to** work. You **had / didn't have to** work. . . .
Permission	We **are / aren't allowed to** speak.	We **were / weren't allowed to** speak.

Must is more formal than *need to* or *have to* and is often used for rules and laws.
Don't have to means that something is not necessary.
Must not means that something is not allowed or is prohibited.
Had to, not *must*, is used to express obligation in the past.
Have to, not *must*, is generally used in questions: *Do you have to leave now?*

Past continuous — Unit 4

Subject	be	Verb + -ing
I	was / wasn't	
You	were / weren't	waiting
He / She / It	was / wasn't	
We / They	were / weren't	

Questions	Answers
Were you waiting?	Yes, I was. / No, I wasn't.
Was she working?	Yes, she was. / No, she wasn't.
What was he doing?	Studying French.
What were they looking at?	The painting.

The past continuous describes actions in progress in the past.
The simple past is often used to show interruption of the action: *We were looking at photographs when our friends arrived.*
The past continuous is also used to set a scene and give background to a story: *It was a dark day. It was raining.*

Comparatives and superlatives · Unit 4

One-syllable adjectives

The red house is **smaller** than the blue house. That's the **biggest** painting in the show.	Add *-er* or *-est* to the adjective: *old nice big small*

Adjectives ending in y

Is the painting **prettier** than the photograph? It's the **prettiest** house in the city.	Change *y* to *i* and add *–er* or *-est*: *happy easy*

Adjectives with two or more syllables

The painting is **more beautiful** than the photograph. The painting is **less realistic** than the photograph. That is the **most beautiful** painting in the store. This is the **least realistic** painting in the artist's collection.	Use *more, most, less,* or *least*: *expensive interesting* *efficient colorful*

as + adjective + as

The photograph is **as colorful as** the painting. The painting isn't **as old as** the photograph.

As + adjective + *as* is used to say that two things are the same or equal. *Not as* + adjective + *as* means that two things are not the same.
Good and *bad* are irregular in the comparative and superlative: *good / better / best; bad / worse / worst.*

Relative clauses (with relative pronoun as subject) · Unit 5

Who is Nicole Shelby? She's a musician **who / that** plays jazz music.	Which CD is hers? It's the CD **that / which** is on the piano.

Relative clauses give more information about a person or thing.
Who is used only for people, *which* only for things. *That* is used for people or things.

Structures with phrasal verbs: Word order · Unit 5

Don't forget to	turn off **the computer.**
Don't forget to	turn **the computer** off.
Don't forget to	turn **it** off

When a phrasal verb is separable, a noun object (e.g. computer) can go either between the verb and the particle or after the particle, but an object pronoun must go between the verb and the particle.
Please pick it up. NOT ~~Please pick up it.~~
Some other separable phrasal verbs are: *put away, pick up, put down, put on, take off.*
The meaning of a phrasal verb is often quite different from the usual meaning of the verb alone.

Present perfect simple / Simple past · Unit 6

Present perfect simple	Simple past
We've lived here **for** four years. I've known Audrey **since** last year. He's had his job **for** a long time.	We moved here four years **ago.** I met Audrey **last year.** He started his job a long time **ago.**

The present perfect simple is used for something that began in the past and continues now. Some verbs that are commonly used with the present perfect simple are *know, be, have,* and *live.*
Ago is used with the simple past. *For* is used with a period of time: *a few minutes, ten days. five years, a month. Since* is used with a starting point: *1995, this morning, last week, 10 o'clock, March 2nd.*

122

Gerunds (as subject and after a preposition)   Unit 6

Gerund as subject

Learning about personality can be interesting.
Taking tests makes me nervous

Gerund after a preposition

Why are you interested **in studying** personality?
Don't be worried **about taking** the test.

A gerund is the –*ing* form of a verb used as a noun.
The -*ing* form in a continuous tense is not called a gerund: *He's reading.*

Tag questions (simple present and simple past)   Unit 7

Affirmative sentence	*Negative sentence*
That story **is** true, **isn't** it?	That story **isn't** true, **is** it?
It **was** a good story, **wasn't** it?	It **wasn't** a good story, **was** it?
That **sounds** like a true story, **doesn't** it?	That **doesn't** sound like a true story, **does** it?
He **gave** her a present, **didn't** he?	He **didn't** give her a present, **did** he?

Tag questions are used to check information or ask for agreement.
If the main verb in the sentence is *be*, *be* is used in the tag. A form of *do* is used with other verbs in the simple present and simple past.
If the sentence is affirmative, the tag is negative. If the sentence is negative, the tag is affirmative.

Future with *will*   Unit 7

Statements	*Yes / No and Wh- questions*	
I / He / She / It will / won't be here soon.	Will she fix it?	Yes, she will. / No, she won't.
We / You / They will / won't fix it.	What will they do?	They'll leave.

Future with *be going to*

Statements	*Yes / No and Wh- questions*	
I'm (not)	Is he going to help?	Yes, he is. / No, he isn't.
He's / She's / It's (isn't) going to help.	Are they going to ?	Yes, they are. / No, they aren't.
We're / You're / They're (aren't)	What are we going to do?	

Will is used for something that is decided at the moment of speaking. It is often used to express an offer: **A**: *We don't have any milk.* **B**: *I'll get some on my way home from work.*
Be going to is used for something that is planned: *Ned's going to help me with my homework tomorrow.*
Both the present continuous and *be going to* are used for planned activities. The meaning is similar, but the present continuous indicates a more fixed (definite) arrangement.

Passive forms   Unit 8

Simple present (is/are + past participle)	*Simple past* (was/were + past participle)
Coffee **is grown** in many countries.	Iced tea **was invented** in the United States.
Cars **are produced** in factories.	Grapes **were grown** there ten years ago.

The passive emphasizes the process or action, not the performer of the action.
A phrase with *by* is used to name the person or thing doing the action: *The sandwich was invented by the Earl of Sandwich in 1762.*

Uses of *the*		Unit 8
	Generalizations without the	**Specific reference with** the
Uncountable	I always put **sugar** in my coffee. They love **music.**	Can you pass **the sugar,** please? Please, turn down **the music.**
Countable	**Cars** are expensive.	Did you put **the car** in the garage?

Quantifiers: *a little, a few, a lot of*		Unit 8
Uncountable	We get **a little** mail every day.	They get **a lot of** mail every day.
Countable	I have **a few** CDs.	Leo has **a lot of** CDs.

Present perfect continuous   Unit 8

Subject	have / has	been + *verb* + -ing
I / You / We / They He / She / It	have / haven't has / hasn't	been traveling.

Questions	Answers
Have you been working?	Yes, I have. / No, I haven't.
Has she been traveling?	Yes, she has. / No, she hasn't.
What has he been doing?	Painting.
Where have they been living?	In San Francisco.

The present perfect continuous is used for actions continuing up to now, especially when we say how long the actions have lasted. It is often used with *for, since,* or expressions like *recently, all day,* or *lately.*
Stative verbs (*know, have, like, love, etc.*) do not take a continuous form:
I've known Cal for a long time. NOT ~~I've been knowing Cal for a long time~~.

Used to + verb   Unit 9

Statements	Questions and answers
I **used to** read about famous explorers. They **didn't use to** travel a lot.	**Did** you **use to** travel a lot? Yes, I **did.** / No, I **didn't.** How **did** people **use to** travel? On horseback.

Used to describes a past state or things that happened regularly in the past. There is no present form. The form *used to* is the same in all persons.

First conditional   Unit 10

If *clause* (Simple present)	Main clause (will + *verb*)
If we win the game,	we'll celebrate.
If Sue doesn't practice,	she won't get better at soccer.

Questions	
If James leaves now,	will he get here on time?
If he's late,	what will we do?

The first conditional describes a real or likely possibility in the future.
It is possible to use other future forms besides *will:* for example, *might, could, be going to.*
It is incorrect to use *will* in the *if* clause: *If we win the game,...* NOT ~~If we will win the game, ...~~
When the *if* clause is the first clause in the sentence, there is a comma at the end of the clause.

Modals and other expressions for advisability		Unit 10
	Affirmative	*Negative*
General advice	You **should** arrive early She **ought to** wear a suit.	We **shouldn't** wear jeans there. . . .
Stronger or urgent advice and warnings	You**'d better** make a good impression. I**'d better** hurry, or I'll be late.	You**'d better not** be late. I**'d better not** take the bus.
What people should do according to rules or law	I**'m supposed to** be there at 11 o'clock. You**'re supposed to** fill out this form.	They**'re not supposed to** leave early. You**'re not supposed to** turn here.

Ought to is not usually used in negatives and questions. *Had better* is not usually used in questions. In negative sentences, the word *not* comes after *had better. Not* comes after *be* in the expression *be supposed to.*

Modals: Possibility (speculation)	Unit 11
Possible	They think the storm **may arrive** tomorrow. Chris **might be** at home now, but he's not answering the phone. This plan **could work**, but I don't want to try it. **Could** this **be** the right answer? I don't know.
Very probable or certain	This **must be** the right trail. Look there's the lake.
Improbable or impossible	It **can't be** true. There's no evidence for it.

Could, not *may* or *might*, is used to speculate with *yes / no* questions.

Reporting commands and requests				Unit 11
With ask *and* tell				
They said, "Please, come on Saturday."	They asked	us	**to come** on Saturday.	
They said, "Don't come on Sunday."	They asked	us	**not to come** on Sunday.	
We said, "Take a break."	We told	them	**to take** a break.	
We said, "Don't work late."	We told	them	**not to work** late.	
With want				
Kate said, "Please, read this article."	Kate wanted	me	**to read** the article	
He said, "Don't put the plant there!"	He **didn't want**	me	**to put** the plant there.	

The negative form with *ask* or *tell* is: *asked / told* + object pronoun + *not* + *to* + verb.
The negative form with *wanted* is: *didn't want* + object + *to* + verb.

Second conditional	Unit 12
If clause (*Simple past*)	**Main clause** (*would + verb*)
If I didn't like the radio program,	I'd ask him to change the station.
If he worked in a different office,	he would take the bus to work.
Questions	
If you didn't have to work,	would you be happy?
What would you do	if you didn't have to work?

The second conditional describes an unreal or imaginary situation that is not true at this time. The past tense does <u>not</u> describe past time. The second conditional refers to the present or future: *If I worked downtown, I'd take the bus to work.* (I don't work downtown and I don't take the bus to work).

Were is often used after *I, he, she,* and *it* in the second conditional especially in formal situations: *If I were you, I'd look for a different job.*

The *if* clause can go at the beginning or end of the sentence. If it is at the beginning, there is a comma at the end of the clause. If it's at the end, no comma is needed.

Indirect questions	Unit 12

Is there a train station near here?
Do you have any idea **if there is** a train station near here?

When does the bus leave?
Can you tell me when the bus **leaves**?

What time does the party start?
Could you tell me what time the party **starts**?

When did the meeting end?
Do you know when the meeting **ended**?

Indirect questions are often used to be polite or if you're not sure the person will know the answer.
The subject and object are not inverted in indirect questions.
The auxiliaries *do / does / did* are not used in indirect questions.
Indirect questions based on *yes / no* questions use *if* in place of the question word.

Irregular Verbs

Base form	Simple past	Past participle	Base form	Simple past	Past participle
be	was/were	been	pay	paid	paid
beat	beat	beaten	put	put	put
become	became	become	quit	quit	quit
bend	bent	bent	read	read	read
break	broke	broken	ride	rode	ridden
buy	bought	bought	ring	rang	rung
cast	cast	cast	rise	rose	risen
choose	chose	chosen	run	ran	run
come	came	come	say	said	said
cut	cut	cut	see	saw	seen
do	did	done	sell	sold	sold
draw	drew	drawn	send	sent	sent
drink	drank	drunk	shoot	shot	shot
drive	drove	driven	show	showed	shown (showed)
eat	ate	eaten	sing	sang	sung
fight	fought	fought	sit	sat	sat
find	found	found	sleep	slept	slept
fit	fit	fit	speak	spoke	spoken
fly	flew	flown	spend	spent	spent
get	got	gotten (got)	stand	stood	stood
give	gave	given	steal	stole	stolen
go	went	gone	sweep	swept	swept
hang	hung	hung	swim	swam	swum
have	had	had	take	took	taken
hide	hid	hidden	teach	taught	taught
hold	held	held	tell	told	told
hurt	hurt	hurt	think	thought	thought
keep	kept	kept	throw	threw	thrown
know	knew	known	understand	understood	understood
lay	laid	laid	unwind	unwound	unwound
lead	led	led	upset	upset	upset
leave	left	left	wake	woke	woken
lend	lent	lent	wear	wore	worn
lose	lost	lost	win	won	won
make	made	made	write	wrote	written
meet	met	met			

Audioscripts

This section provides audioscripts where a reference and extra support for recorded activities may be helpful.

UNIT 1

3b

1
- A: Do you like to ski a lot?
- B: Yes, I do.
- A: So do I.

2
- A: What are you doing?
- B: I'm relaxing. I had a hard day.
- A: So did I!

3
- A: Did you go out last night?
- B: No, I didn't.
- A: I did. I had a good time.

4
- A: Have you ever been to Scotland?
- B: No, I haven't.
- A: Neither have I, but I'd like to go.

4b

A = Adam, J = Jessica
- A: Hi, you're at the conference too, aren't you?
- J: Yes, I am.
- A: I thought I recognized you. My name's Adam…Adam Garcia.
- J: Hi, Adam. I'm Jessica Spicer. Isn't this hotel nice?
- A: Yes, it is. I'm so glad it has a gym.
- J: So am I. I really needed to unwind! It was a long day.
- A: Yes, it was, but it was interesting, too. There were some good presentations.
- J: Yes, there were.
- A: Do you walk a lot?
- J: Yes, but normally I walk outside. I don't usually use a treadmill.
- A: Neither do I. I live near a park, so I walk there a lot.
- J: Where do you live?
- A: Vancouver, Canada.
- J: Oh, I've always wanted to go there. What's it like?
- A: It's nice. It's a beautiful city and it's really easy to get out and do things. I love doing things outdoors.
- J: So do I.
- A: Where are you from?
- J: Arizona…Tempe, Arizona.
- A: Where exactly is Tempe?
- J: It's not far from Phoenix. Do you know where that is?
- A: Hmmm. Yes, I think so. So, what do you do?
- J: I'm in sales. I work for a small computer company. What about you?
- A: I'm in sales too. I work for X-Tech.
- J: Oh, yes. I know that company. Well, that's enough for me today. It was nice talking to you.
- A: Yes, it was nice talking to you, too. I'll probably see you tomorrow.
- J: OK, see you.

5b

1
- A: What do you do?
- B: I'm a graphic designer. What about you?
- A: I'm a computer programmer.

2
- A: What do you do in your free time?
- B: I like scuba diving.
- A: Oh, so do I!

3
- A: Where do you live?
- B: In Mexico City.
- A: What's Mexico City like?
- B: It's beautiful.

4
- A: It was nice to meet you.
- B: Nice to meet you, too.

11b

1 Being a kid can be lots of fun. You play a lot—you have a lot of games that Mom and Dad don't know how to play. I love playing soccer…I get a lot of time to play soccer as a kid. Adults don't have as much time to play—my dad works so he doesn't get to play soccer very much. One bad thing about being a kid is school…I don't really like going to school. I can't stand doing chores either…especially cleaning my room. Oh, and, my brother has a new trumpet…that's really annoying because he isn't very good at playing it!

2 Some good things about being a kid are: summer vacation, playing sports, and getting lots of presents on my birthday—adults don't get as many presents. I like playing with my friends every weekend, too. Bad things about being a kid are: some of the chores I have to do—I don't mind doing some of them, but there are some I can't stand, like doing dishes. Sometimes I can't watch TV when my dad wants to watch a program that I can't watch…I don't like that. And, I don't like doing homework. But, I'm happy I don't have to pay taxes! That's one bad thing about being an adult.

3 I don't like having to go to bed so early…at seven-thirty. I always have to finish all the food on my plate, even if I don't like it…yuck. One thing I really don't like…I don't like older people telling me what to do. That's probably the worst thing about being a kid. There are a lot of good things though… I don't have to work and my parents give me money for allowance… when I'm an adult, I'll have to pay for everything. And, I get to see my friends all the time at school… we have recess so we can play. You don't have recess when you're an adult!

UNIT 2
4b

Silvia

I like *hectic* just because of the sound. And, I like *forward* because of its meaning.

Victor

I like *imagination* for both its meaning and its sound.

Fabiana

My favorite word is *strength* because it only has one vowel and seven consonants. I like to pronounce *strength* and I like its meaning, too.

Takahiro

I love the word *flabbergasted*. I think it's because it's almost like you can see what it means, as if it shows the very surprised face of a person who is flabbergasted. You can almost see the person's mouth dropping open, with their eyes wide open.

Anna

I like *happiness* and *fabulous* for their meanings. I have one phrase—not just a word—that I like…it's that something doesn't "come easy." When I was first learning English, I thought this was one word and I looked for it in the dictionary as one word. Of course I couldn't find it. I guess that just means that learning English doesn't always come easy!

Alfredo

I like *curiosity* because of the sound of it…and the meaning, too. I think curiosity is a good thing…but I also love the expression "Curiosity killed the cat." It's funny to say that <u>too much</u> curiosity can be a bad thing.

7a

V = Victor, S = Silvia

V: What does this word mean? *Flabb*…?
S: *Flabbergasted*? It means very, very surprised.
V: How do you pronounce it? *Flabbergasted*?
S: Yes, that's right. It has four syllables.
V: Is it a noun?
S: Victor! No, it's an adjective.
V: Oh, yes!… Is it a formal word?
S: No, not really. I think people mainly use it in speaking…. No, I don't think it's a word you'd hear someone use in a really formal situation.

10b

I = Interviewer, S = Sandra

I: Can you explain a little about your experience of synesthesia?
S: It was mainly something I experienced as a child. If I really concentrate, I still have the experience now, but the real experience of it was as a child.
I: How did you experience it? Which senses were affected?
S: It was only related to the days of the week. Each day of the week has a specific color.
I: For example?
S: Well, Monday is a combination of brown and lilac…kind of like clouds of the two colors coming together. And, Tuesday is blue…not really a dark blue though, brighter than that….
I: It seems like the colors are really specific for you, lilac rather than just purple or a particular shade of blue rather than just any blue.
S: Yes, that's right. And, the way I see Wednesday is even more specific—it's the only day that has an image with it.
I: Can you describe it?
S: Yes, it's like a dark red curtain…dark, but not a gloomy red and the curtain is velvet. And there's a stage in front of the curtain. And, in front of that is my ballet teacher. I took ballet lessons when I was 3 or 4 years old and that teacher is standing in front of the red curtain… and she's always standing in the same way.
I: That's interesting. Do you think there's any reason why you have such a specific image for Wednesday?
S: No, not at all. In fact, my ballet lessons were on Saturdays, so there's no reason for an association with Wednesday.
I: What about the other days of the week?
S: Thursday, Friday, and Saturday are only colors for me. There are no images or shapes with them. Thursday is orange, Friday is yellow…a bright, sunny yellow…, and then Saturday is gray.
I: And Sunday?
S: Sunday is red again—like Wednesday but there's no image. There is a shape though…it's a rectangle.
I: Hmm, a rectangle... So, do you remember how you felt about having these experiences then?
S: Yes, I thought it was quite nice. The only thing I thought was, "Oh, Saturday is gray." I didn't like it…it probably reminded me of rainy skies or something.
I: And how do you feel about it now?
S: I think it would be great fun to experience more of it now. For example, I would love to feel that music had color…

UNIT 3
1b

I = Interviewer, J = Jennifer

I: Jennifer, tell us about your work in movie-making.
J: I don't work for a film company, I work independently. I've done writing and directing mainly. I've written one screenplay that was made into a feature film and I directed that.
I: So, you've already written and directed one movie. That's impressive. Do you do it full-time?
J: No, not yet. I have a day job to support myself…. I still haven't quit that, but I hope to someday.
I: Was it hard to get started?
J: Yes, it was…I went to film school and then I had a lot of pretty low-level jobs…. It was hard to find time to write in those kinds of jobs, but I finally managed to finish the screenplay for my movie.
I: What do you do after you write a screenplay?
J: Well, you have to get money to actually make the movie. Then, there's casting—choosing the actors—and then actually "shooting" or filming the movie. After that, you edit it. And then finally, you hope to sell the movie to someone.
I: It sounds like a long process.
J: It is…it took about four years to make my movie.
I: What were the most interesting parts of the process for you?
J: Well, casting was really interesting, but it can be frustrating, too. If you want to try and get a well-known Hollywood actor, it can mean a lot of waiting for each person's response. We ended up choosing an unknown actress for my movie because none of the famous ones could work with our schedule. But, I don't think I'd do it that way again…a famous actress can make a big difference, so I think I'd wait.

I: What was the best part of the process?

J: Oh, definitely shooting the movie. It's <u>extremely</u> tiring—we worked 12 to 14 hours a day for four weeks on my movie—but it's also very exciting. It's so different from any other kind of job!

I: And, what's next for you?

J: Well, I have a lot of ideas for movies…some I haven't worked on yet and others are in progress. I finished another screenplay a few weeks ago…. Otherwise, I'd like to do some film editing…I haven't really done a lot of editing yet and I'd like to.

5a

E = Eddie, M = Maxine

E: That movie was really good!

M: Hmm. Do you think so?

E: What? Didn't you like it?

M: Well, it was OK. But if you ask me, it was a little unrealistic.

E: I don't think it was…. OK, maybe a little, but I think the acting was good.

M: I guess so. I just don't think they make thrillers like they used to. I always like the old-fashioned thrillers, you know, the classics.

E: I like them too. I suppose you're right, but I still don't think this movie was too bad.

M: OK, let's agree to disagree on this one.

8b

C = Charlie, W = Woman, M = Man

W: Charlie, you've been an extra on a TV show… what was it like?

C: Well, it's not actually as glamorous as you might think. You need to be patient—you sit around doing nothing and waiting a lot.

W: Really? I thought it would be really busy and exciting the whole time.

C: Not really…maybe it would be if you were a star on a show, but when you're an extra you're not in every scene…you know, you're just a background person…so there's a lot of waiting between scenes. But, it's really interesting when you're actually doing a scene.

M: How many shows have you been in?

C: Just two. They were both dramas.

W: What kinds of things did you have to do?

C: Well, mainly just stand around or walk around, depending on the scene. One scene was at a party so we had to stand around talking. But, we weren't actually allowed to speak—they didn't want the microphones to pick any noise up, so we had to pretend to speak.

W: Hmm, that's interesting.

M: Did you get to meet any stars?

C: Well, yes…it was kind of funny. I was standing there in one scene when the director said, "Hey, you…the tall guy with the dark curly hair. Move into the background."

W: And that was you?

C: Yes, I had to move because they said I looked too much like the star of the show. He was tall with dark curly hair, too. They thought it might be confusing for people watching.

M: So you got to meet him?

C: Yeah, he was nice. He thought it was funny that we looked similar. He came up to me later and said he'd call me if he was sick. He never did call though!

W: That's too bad. Being an extra sounds like fun.

C: It was. I'd definitely do it again. I'd love to be in a sitcom.

W: So…you look like a TV star…hmm, I never noticed…

UNIT 4

1b

H = Hugh, K = Kristy

H: Aren't these pictures great? They bring back a lot of memories.

K: Yes, they do. Look at this one…wasn't this the surprise party we had for you?

H: Yes, it was…what a good party…

K: Of course, you almost ruined the surprise.

H: I did not!

K: Yes, you did. Don't you remember? You went out and we were getting ready for the party while you were gone…but you came back early…

H: I did? I don't remember that….

K: Yes, we were just finishing the decorations when you came in. We all jumped up and shouted "Surprise!" …but we weren't exactly ready for you to get home.

H: I don't think I even realized that…all I remember is that it was a really nice party and I had a lot of fun.

K: What's this?

H: This was the day I moved into my first apartment…everyone came over and helped me move…weren't you there?

K: No, I don't think so. I think I went away that weekend…Who's this?

H: That's Kenny.

K: Really? I don't even recognize him. What was going on in this picture?

H: We were trying to get my painting up the stairs. It was really big and heavy. We finally did it, but it took a really long time…Oh, look! Here's a picture of our ski trip…do you remember that?

K: Of course I do! I fell and hurt my ankle the first day and spent the rest of the trip in the lodge!

H: Oh, I'd forgotten about that. What happened?

K: It was kind of embarrassing really…I wasn't even skiing, I was just standing at the top of the mountain and some guy ran into me!

H: Oh, that's right. That was really bad luck, wasn't it?

K: I'll say!

8c

Now here's an interesting story about the mystery of how memory works…or doesn't work.

Give Tatiana Cooley 100 faces and names to memorize and she can remember 70 of them 15 minutes later. Give her 4,000 numbers or 500 words and she'll repeat them better than most people. It's the same with a 54-line poem. So, why does Tatiana Cooley need sticky notes?

She says she's incredibly absent-minded! She recently defeated 16 challengers to keep her memory champion title, but when asked how many brothers and sisters she has, she replied, "Six…er…seven…er six."

She keeps a daily To Do list and says she "lives by reminder notes." According to Tatiana, the ability to memorize things is different from remembering things on a daily basis. She says her memorizing is "not on the same level as remembering to call people."

Tatiana insists that she is not unique. She believes that anybody can train their mind to memorize. She uses two techniques: visualization and association. For visualization, she looks at material and mentally photographs it. For association, she makes up a story to link random numbers and words.

Tatiana noticed that her ability to memorize was better than average when she was studying in college. She found that taking lecture notes was enough to prepare for tests. She didn't have to do anything else.

Tatiana gives credit for her abilities to her mother and father. They only allowed her to watch news and educational programs on TV when she was growing up. They played games to help her memory and encouraged her to read and learn languages. She reads in Portuguese, Spanish, and French. She thinks memorization is fun. She says, "I've always loved to learn. I've been like a sponge my whole life."

So, there you go, folks, it's reassuring to know that even a memory champion needs a little help remembering everyday things sometimes. And, our next story is...

10a

C = Cindy, M = Meg

C: Do you remember the name of that little Italian restaurant on Third Street?
M: Which one?
C: You know...the one we went to for Isabelle's birthday a few weeks ago?
M: Oh yes, I know the one you mean. It's really nice, but I can't remember the name either.
C: I think it begins with a G. Oh, it's on the tip of my tongue, but I can't think of it.
M: Is it something like Gianni's or Gino's?
C: No, I don't think so. It'll come to me in a minute.
M: Try not to think about it and you'll probably remember. That always works for me.
C: Maybe you're right. But, remind me to ask Isabelle just in case. I'd like to go there for dinner next weekend.
M: OK.

UNIT 5

3a

1	a wooden guitar	5	a glass window
2	a gold necklace	6	leather shoes
3	a diamond ring	7	a cotton T-shirt
4	a silver coin	8	a metal clothes hanger

4b

Mauricio:
Something that's important to me...hmm...let's see. I think it would have to be my motorcycle and backpack. I use my motorcycle to go to work and almost everywhere else. I carry everything I need in my backpack so that's really important, too. I don't think I could manage without either one of them.

Elaine:
I have a ring that was my grandmother's. It's my most important and favorite possession. It's a beautiful gold ring that has a diamond on it. My grandfather gave it to my grandmother, then she gave it to my mother, and my mother gave it to me a few years ago. It's really special...I hardly ever wear it though because I don't want to lose it.

Ruth:
Lars and I have a basket that has all our family memories in it. Photographs, letters, pictures, and art that our children made. It really is our family history. Our children don't really appreciate how important it is right now, but I think they will when they're older.

Bruce:
That's easy. My stereo and CD collection are my most important things. It's a good stereo and I had to save a long time to be able to buy it. I have at least 100 CDs in my collection. I collect music from around the world. I just love music that is interesting or unusual. My friends always know what to give me for my birthday...a new CD always makes me happy.

Mia:
A watch that was my mother's. It isn't expensive and it's a little old-fashioned...it's gold and it has a leather band...but I really like it. People always notice it when I wear it. They always ask where I got it.

6a

K = Ken, L = Lily

K: What's the matter?
L: I'm fixing this picture frame, but I need something to turn this little thing.
K: Do you want a screwdriver?
L: No, it's like a screwdriver, but it's smaller. You use it to turn really small screws. I'm not sure what it's called.
K: Is this it? It looks like a really small screwdriver.
L: Yes, that's it. Thanks.
K: You know, I think this is just another kind of screwdriver.
L: Oh really? Well, whatever it is, I fixed the picture frame with it!

8b

I = Ingrid, N = Neal

I: What's the matter, Neal?
N: This toaster oven drives me crazy. I can never figure it out. It has all these buttons and dials, but when I push a button or turn a dial, it doesn't do what I expect it to.
I: It doesn't look that complicated. Let me see. What are you trying to do?
N: I want to toast this sandwich.
I: OK, so here's the temperature dial...let's turn it to "medium."
N: OK, then what?
I: Well, we just turn the oven on. Hmm...it must be this button here, it says "on/off" right?
N: I guess, but what's this other button that says "toast"?
I: I have no idea.... Don't touch it...let's just ignore it.
N: OK, but it doesn't seem to be getting hot. Are you sure it's turned on?
I: Yes, it's turned on.
N: I'm going to turn it up.
I: Don't turn it up, it'll get too hot! Be patient. It takes a minute to heat up. See, now it's starting to get warm. We'll have a cup of coffee and the sandwich will be ready in a few minutes. So, what did you think of the new project ideas?

N: Hey, it smells like something's burning. My sandwich! Quick! Take it out and turn off the oven.
I: OK...whoops, I think it's a little too late. It's really black. You might just want to throw it away.
N: No, no, it's OK, I'll eat it.... I told you that toaster oven wasn't easy to work.
I: I guess you're right. Maybe you should start bringing something you can microwave.
N: Maybe I should...

UNIT 6

4a

Russell:

Well, most of my friends are from work. I didn't live here before I got this job, so I met most of the friends I have now through work. Audrey is the first person I met here…so I've known her for two years. We socialize a lot outside work, but I also have a lot of friends in other departments. I play basketball with some guys from accounting, and then we have an office soccer team, too. We get together almost every weekend to play. I have one old friend, Gary, who I kind of keep in touch with, but he lives in a different city, and we don't see each other that often. I haven't seen him since his wedding, so that's about two years. He's one of my oldest and best friends, but it's hard to stay in touch sometimes. So, my friends these days are mainly from work…and that's fine. It's more practical since we spend so much time together anyway.

Audrey:

My social life is definitely separate from work. Russell is really the only friend I have from my job. He and I get along really well, so we see each other outside work, but otherwise I don't socialize with people from work unless I have to. I've lived in this city all my life, so I've had most of my friends for a long time. I've known my best friend, Lisa, since I was six years old—we lived in the same apartment building as children—so that's about 20 years now. I'm also a musician…I play the guitar in a band and a lot of my friends are musicians. I've been in the same band for three years now and the other band members are my really good friends. I think it's good to know different kinds of people and I don't want my whole life to be about work, so I guess that's why I try to have a lot of different friends.

6a

A = Annie, D = Daniel, P = Philip

D: Hi, Annie. I haven't seen you for ages!
A: Oh hi, Daniel. It's good to see you.
D: Annie, this is my friend Philip. We work in the same office. Annie is a friend from my hiking club.
A: Hi, Philip. It's nice to meet you.
P: Hi. Nice to meet you, too. You know…you look familiar Annie. Have we met before?
A: I'm not sure. You look kind of familiar, too.
P: Do you work at the central library?
A: Yes, I've worked there for a long time.
P: Oh, that's why I recognize you. I go there a lot.

9b

I = Interviewer, DW = Damon Wheeler

I: Good morning. Today we're talking about personality testing. Our guest is Damon Wheeler, who researches personality and personality assessment. Mr. Wheeler, there are a lot of different kinds of personality tests out there these days, aren't there?
DW: Yes, there really are. If you look on the Internet, you can find all kinds of tests. Some of them are pretty scientific. For example, written personality tests might be used for medical purposes or by employers who want to know more about potential employees. And, there are also lots of others: color tests, food quizzes, graphology…
I: Graphology is related to handwriting, right?
DW: Yes, exactly. It's the study of handwriting to learn about personality. Some people take it very seriously. There are some employers that use it in the workplace. Other

people use it to see if they're compatible with a boyfriend or girlfriend.
I: How accurate are personality tests?
DW: Well, it depends on the kind of test. Some tests are more scientific than others. It's hard to know how accurate they are. Personality is so complicated. It's hard to say if one test could tell you everything about personality. There are some ways of testing that people don't accept anymore…for example, phrenology.
I: What's phrenology?
DW: It was used in the 18th and 19th centuries. Basically, people thought that you could learn about personality by feeling the bumps on a person's head.
I: Really? By touching a person's head?
DW: Yes, it seems strange now, but a lot of doctors and well-educated people believed in it at the time.
I: That is hard to believe. Why do you think people are so interested in personality testing?
DW: I think there are different reasons. Obviously, there are medical situations where tests can be useful, and as I said, some employers use them in the workplace. I think people also use personality tests to try and learn more about themselves and the people around them…

11b

unfriendly	disorganized	impatient
unenthusiastic	disagreeable	impolite
unkind	dishonest	
unpopular		
unintelligent		

UNIT 7

1b

W = Woman, M = Man

W: I rented a good movie last night.
M: Really. What was it?
W: It was called "It Could Happen to You." It's about a policeman and a waitress. The policeman won the lottery and—
M: He gave the waitress half his winnings, didn't he?
W: Yes, he did. How did you know? Have you seen the movie?
M: No, but I've read about it. The movie was based on a true story, wasn't it?
W: Really? I didn't know that. I thought it was just a movie.
M: No, I'm pretty sure it was a true story. I think it was a police officer in New York…he went to this Italian restaurant a lot and he got to know this one waitress. One night, instead of a tip, he offered her half his share in a lottery ticket. You know, it was kind of a joke…but they chose the numbers together. Of course, the waitress just forgot about it. But, the police officer came back the next day and said that they'd won—six million dollars!
W: Wow, that's amazing, isn't it?
M: Yes, it is. I don't know if everyone would keep a promise like that to share the winnings.
W: Hmm, you're probably right…. The story in the movie is a little different because in the movie the policeman and the waitress didn't know each other—it was the first time that he'd been in the restaurant. And, he already had the ticket…so they didn't choose the numbers together.
M: Yes, I think that is different from the original story.
W: Also, the waitress had huge financial problems in the

W: Also, the waitress had huge financial problems in the movie...she worked hard and saved, but she didn't earn a lot of money. So, it was all perfect...and, of course, she and the police officer fell in love in the end...I don't think that happened in real life...

M: No, that sounds more like a Hollywood ending, doesn't it?

W: Yes, it does...but you never know.

6a

1

A: Can we have the check, please?

B: Yes, here you are.

A: Let me get this.

C: No, it's my treat.

A: It's too expensive.

C: You paid last time. This is on me.

A: Well, OK. Thank you.

C: You're welcome.

2

A: Can I help you?

B: Can I cash this check, please?

A: Of course. Can I see some identification, please?

B: Yes, here's my driver's license.

A: OK. How would you like it? In tens or twenties?

B: Tens please.

A: Here you are.

B: Thank you.

A: You're welcome.

7b

I = Interviewer, L = Luke

I: So, Luke, you trade with people...you barter?

L: Yes, I do it a little less now, but I've done it a lot in the past...basically all my working life.

I: How did you get started?

L: Well, I had this friend and she bartered for everything...she's a cook and a hairdresser. We started trading...I made some furniture for her and she cut my hair and made some meals for me...and then I just kept doing it.

I: Is it hard to find people to barter with?

L: Not for me. I have a regular job as a house painter and I know a lot of people...if I need something, I just ask around.

I: And how do you arrange it?

L: We figure out how many hours of work is a fair exchange. Sometimes it's hard to decide, but it's important to agree on everything before you start. Otherwise, you can have problems.

I: Have you had any bad experiences?

L: Really only one or two in twelve years. The worst experience was with someone who was going to fix my computer. We didn't agree on anything in advance and in the end he wanted too much in return...he wanted me to paint his whole house!... I paid him cash to get it over with.

I: What else have you bartered for?

L: Let's see...furniture, car repairs...even a truck once. I helped some friends paint and fix up their house and they gave me a nice old truck that I actually still use.

I: You must really like to barter.

L: I do. It's a good option for people who don't have a lot of money. And, I just enjoy it.... Actually, I would love to trade for everything, but I have to start doing less. I'm bartering too much and not making enough money. You have to make some money!

8b

make money	make friends
do someone's hair	make a decision
make a profit	do laundry
make a mistake	make a list
do a job	make noise
make a living	do the shopping
do someone a favor	make a meal
do housework or chores	do business

UNIT 8

3b

TG = Tour Guide

TG: Good morning and welcome to the factory. This is one of our main production sites for making potato chips. Potato chips are the largest-selling snack chip in the United States.... Here is our delivery area. Can anyone guess how many potatoes we use in a year?

Various voices: Hmm, maybe a million?... No idea.... Probably a lot.

TG: About a hundred thirty million pounds of potatoes are used in a year to make more than 35 million pounds of potato chips.

Tourist voice: What were those numbers again?

TG: A hundred thirty million pounds of potatoes to make 35 million pounds of chips...

TG: This is where the potatoes are delivered. Our potatoes come from eight different states, as well as Canada. We order them so that they arrive as fresh as possible and we have very specific guidelines for the potatoes we accept. Before they are unloaded, each load is tested for size, color, and overall condition. About 1% of the potatoes are rejected.

TG: This is where the potatoes are cleaned and peeled. They go through this machine and they are inspected for quality again. After that, they go into the cutting machine where they are cut into thin slices. Again, we have specific guidelines for the size and shape of the potato slices, so any that aren't the right size are taken out...

TG: And now the potatoes are ready for cooking. The potato slices are fried quickly to make them crisp. After they're cooked, the chips are salted and cooled. Then, special seasonings are added.

Different tourist voice: How many different flavors are there?

TG: Right now we have ten flavors, but our best-selling chip is still the regular salted kind...

TG: The cooked chips come here for packaging. They're weighed and put into bags. Then they're put into cases for shipping. That's the process from potato to potato chip.... And now we have the best part of the tour...where you can taste some of our delicious chips...

4c

Apple pie

Peel 8 or 9 apples. Then slice them. Add 2 cups sugar and 1 teaspoon cinnamon and mix well. Put mixture in pie shell. Bake in oven for 45 minutes.

Egg salad

Boil 4 eggs in water. Peel the cooked eggs and chop them into small pieces. Add mayonnaise, salt, and pepper. Mix well. Cover and chill.

7a

A: I just read this book about tea.

B: Was it interesting?

A: Yes, it was. Did you know that—apart from water—more tea is consumed around the world than any other beverage?

B: Hmm, I didn't know that.

A: And, do you know how people started drinking tea?

B: I have no idea.

A: Well, there was an emperor in China more than 5000 years ago. He boiled his water because he realized that it was safer. According to the legend, one day he was boiling some water under a tree and some leaves fell in. He decided to taste it and because of that, we have tea! That's the story anyway.

B: Well, that explains a lot… Aren't we lucky he was sitting under the right kind of tree?

8b-c

Once upon a time there was a king who had three daughters. He wanted to choose one of them to be the queen. He called the daughters to him and said, "My dear children, I love all three of you dearly and for a long time I have not known which one of you to name as queen. Now I have decided. The one who brings me a birthday present which is most necessary to human life shall be queen. Go and make your plans."

The king's birthday arrived. The two oldest daughters brought him presents that were very necessary, but were also very, very expensive. However, the youngest daughter only brought him a small pile of salt. When the king saw her present, he became very angry. He told the daughter to leave his castle and never come back.

The daughter left her father's castle. She had nowhere to go. She wandered in the forest and was very hungry and cold. As she walked along one day, a prince saw her and fell in love with her at once. She agreed to marry him and a great party was planned at the prince's castle. The king was invited, but he did not know that the bride was his daughter.

Well, the girl told the cook to make all the dishes for the party with no salt. At the wedding, everyone started eating and they found that the food had no taste. One guest said, "There is no salt in the meat." Then, everyone started saying, "There is no salt in the meat."

Then, the king said very sadly, "Truly, I now know how necessary salt is. But, because I didn't know that before, I sent my own daughter away and I will never see her again."

When the daughter heard this, she went to the king and made herself known. They all lived happily ever after.

UNIT 9
3a

1 I was going to Japan on a business trip. I mailed my passport to the passport office to get a visa. Unfortunately, my passport—with the new visa—was stolen from a mail truck on its return. I had to cancel my trip at the last minute, get a new passport, and start the process all over. I ended up going on the trip a month later. So my worst travel experience was before my trip even started!

2 My friend and I were on vacation in Ireland. We were driving around, taking pictures, and sightseeing, and we saw a poem posted on the wall of a restaurant. We'd never heard of the poet, but we loved the poem. That night, we stopped in a little village and we started talking to a man in a crowded pub. We told him about the poem in the restaurant. He knew the poem, but more surprisingly, he said, "The poet who wrote it is right over there. Do you want to meet him?" It was wonderful!

3 I was hitchhiking with a friend in California. We stood in the same spot for ages because no one was driving past. It was getting late and we were absolutely freezing. Finally, this man stopped, but not to give us a ride—he invited us to his house up the road so that we could get warm. So, we went to his house and his wife gave us a delicious hot meal. That was years ago, but it's my best travel memory.

4 My friend and I were traveling in the Czech Republic. We bought train tickets to go back to Prague. It was only supposed to be a 45-minute ride. During the ride we heard announcements but couldn't understand them. After about an hour, we started wondering why it was taking so long…so we asked the train conductor. He started to laugh…he said we should have gotten off and changed trains somewhere. By that point, we were very close to the border of Germany! We got off in a small town and had to wait for a train back to Prague. The whole trip took 6 hours—almost the same amount of time it took to fly from New York to Prague!

7a

C = Charles Santos, H = Hotel Receptionist

C: Hi, I have a reservation. The name is Santos, Charles Santos.

H: Oh, yes, Mr. Santos. How many nights are you staying?

C: Three.

H: And, you wanted a single room?

C: No, I asked for a double room.

H: Oh, sorry. We can change that. Can you fill out this form, please?

C: Of course.

H: Can I have your credit card, please?

C: Yes, here it is.

H: Here are your keys.

C: Thank you.

A: Good morning. Can I help you?

B: Yes, I have a ticket for a flight from Seattle to San Diego on Sunday, May 11th. Is it possible to change my flight to another day?

A: Let's see. There's a $75 charge to change this ticket. Is that OK?

B: Yes, that's fine. Here's my credit card.

A: Thank you. When would you like to fly?

B: On Sunday, June 1st.

A: Hmm, there's a flight at 9:00 a.m. on June 1st. And there's one at 1:30 p.m. Which would you like?

B: The one at 1:30, please.

A: …OK…here's your new ticket. It's a good idea to call and confirm the flight the day before.

B: OK, thank you.

A: You're welcome.

11b

I = Interviewer, A = Annelise

I: Our topic today is adventure and exploration…. A good vacation for many of us is a relaxing week in a beautiful setting. But others look for adventure and excitement all the time. Annelise Morgan is one of those people. She's made a career out of adventure travel and exploration—she's climbed mountains in North and South America, as well as Asia, she's sailed across the Pacific Ocean, and she's walked across deserts in Australia and Africa…. Annelise, tell us how you got started.

A: It started when I was a kid…I used to read about all the famous explorers…you know, polar explorers like Amundsen and Shackleton…and Lewis and Clark who explored unmapped areas of the United States. I was also interested in the early women explorers...

I: Were there many women explorers back then?

A: Well, obviously not many, but there were a few...it wasn't easy...some women explorers even used to wear men's clothing to disguise themselves.

I: Really?

A: Yes, it's remarkable when you think of it...but, really, I find any early exploration—by women or men—just amazing...think of the difficulties and the hardship! We have all this high-tech equipment nowadays that we consider absolutely essential. Early travelers and explorers just didn't have any of it...and they still managed to explore so much.

I: I guess I hadn't really thought about that.

A: Yes...now we have fabric and clothes that keep us warm and dry all the time...or cool and dry if we're in a hot place.... We have light-weight equipment...and then, of course, there are things like satellite phones. Early explorers didn't use to have anything like that. If you think about how they used to travel—heavy clothes and equipment, slow transportation, almost no safety equipment—it makes their achievements even more impressive.

I: Well, your achievements are pretty impressive, too.

A: Well...maybe... The fact is that no high-tech equipment will take away all the risk of certain kinds of exploration and travel...but that's what makes it exciting. That's why people still do it and will continue to do it.

I: Yes, and speaking of that, tell us about your next trip...

UNIT 10

1b-c

B = Bob, V = Valerie

B: And, finally, here's Valerie with a story about just how superstitious some of you athletes and sports fans can be.

V: They announced today that a Canadian coin buried under the ice at the hockey rink in the last Olympics will be taken to the hockey hall of fame.... The ice keepers for the rink were from Canada and they secretly buried the coin before the games.... Well, Canada won, so since then, athletes have been visiting the rink...lining up to look at the coin and touch it. They all hope it will bring them good luck in their games.

B: Hmm, that's interesting. What do you think, Valerie? Could a coin really be that lucky?

V: I don't know...since Canada won the gold medals in both men's and women's hockey, it isn't surprising that many people believe the coin brought the Canadians good luck.

B: You know...I think athletes are often a pretty superstitious group. I know there are a lot of superstitions in baseball.

V: Really? For example?

B: Well, it's good luck to put gum on your hat.... And, you never lend your bat to a teammate; if you do that, you'll have bad luck.... Oh, here's another good one.... It's bad luck if a dog walks across the field before a game begins.

V: And then there's rodeo riding...

B: Rodeo riding?

V: Yes, there are a lot of superstitions in rodeo riding. It's bad luck to wear yellow. It's bad luck to put your hat on a bed; if you do, you might get injured.... And, there's a money superstition, too.... You don't carry coins in your pocket; if you do, you won't win a lot of money.

B: Now that's interesting because in golf, it's good luck to

carry coins when you play.

V: Well, there you go...one person's bad luck is another person's good luck!

B: I guess! So, how do you know so much about rodeo riding anyway, Valerie?

V: Now that's a long story that we don't have time for today!

4a-b

H = Harry, M = Michele

H: Oh, no. It's going to be hard to find a parking space today.

M: Don't worry. I've got the parking tiger.

H: The what?

M: The parking tiger. Look, the head moves when you press the button. Now we'll find a parking space in a few minutes.

H: Oh, come on, Michele! That's too much.

M: No, I really believe it works.

H: That's silly.

M: Do you mean you don't have any little superstitions like this...you never carry a lucky charm or anything?

H: Well...if I hear a certain song on the radio, then I always think it will be a good day. And, I have a lucky tie that I always wear for important meetings.

M: So, you're a little superstitious then, aren't you?

H: Well...only a little. Hey! There's a parking spot!

M: See, I told you—it really works!

11a-b

Person 1:

It was my very first real job.... I was about 20 and just out of school. I started working in an office...it wasn't difficult, but I was nervous and I wanted to do a good job. A new boss had just taken over. I hadn't actually met her yet...I'd seen her around the office and I have to say she didn't look very approachable...she dressed very formally and it didn't seem like she smiled much or chatted with people. Anyway, I was taking some files to her...I walked into her office and immediately dropped the files all over the floor. As I was desperately trying to pick them all up, I bumped into her desk and spilled coffee all over it...it was awful and she was just staring at me...I thought I was going to have to look for a new job for sure!... Then, suddenly, she started laughing! We both started laughing and then she told me to sit down. We chatted for a while and she actually wanted me to take on more responsibility. It turned out that she was a really nice, warm person...in fact, she's still a good friend of mine. It just goes to show how wrong first impressions can be...

Person 2:

It was years ago...my sister and I took a drive out in the country...we were way out in the country, miles from anything when we got a flat tire...we pulled over and got out of the car...we were young and neither one of us had any idea how to fix a flat...as we were standing there, wondering what to do, a gang of eight or ten men on motorcycles roared over the hill and stopped right in front of us...we were scared to death—we were thinking of all the TV shows and movies where men on motorcycles were bad guys! The leader of the group got off his bike and came over, followed by three big, rough-looking men...he didn't smile or anything, he just looked at us and said "Give me your keys"...we were terrified, but my sister handed over the keys...then, we watched as the four men changed our tire for us. When they finished, the leader gave us back the keys and said, "Now go home," and they got on their motorcycles and roared off...ever since then, I have tried not to judge people by how they look.

UNIT 11

3a-b

N = Nina, B = Ben, S = Stuart

N: Your garden is so beautiful, Ben. It must be a lot of work.

B: Not really. I enjoy working in the garden. I think it's good to be outside in nature.

S: I read an interesting article recently about a professor who would agree with you.

B: Really?

S: Yes, he's doing research into how contact with nature and natural environments might have positive health benefits...and could even help prevent illness.

B: It makes sense to me.

S: Yes, that's what he says...that many people instinctively feel healthier when they're in a beautiful landscape, for example. But, the professor says that doctors and the medical world don't recognize this possibility. He feels they should because it could be beneficial. So, he's trying to get more solid evidence together.

N: I know there's been research on the positive effects of animals and pets on health...you know, that having a dog or cat is good for your health.

S: Yes, he mentions that, but I was surprised at how much focus there was on plants, too...he believes that contact with plants—from gardening to even just looking at trees—could help people get well.

N: Really? Isn't that a little much?

S: Well, there does seem to be some evidence for it...in one study, patients in a hospital who had a view of trees had shorter hospital stays than patients who only had a view of a brick wall. And in another study, office employees reported that having plants in their workplace made them feel calmer.

B: I know I always feel calmer after I've been working in the garden...so it must be good for me!

N: Well, I won't complain if my doctor tells me to take a vacation in a beautiful place for my health!

S: No, I won't either.

7a-b

H1 = Hiker 1, H2 = Hiker 2, H3 = Hiker 3

H1: Hi!

H2: Hi. Can you help us? We wanted to go to the Windy Lake Trail, but I think we're lost.

H1: You missed the turn. It's back that way.

H2: Oh, no! Another hiker told us to come up this trail.

H1: It happens a lot. It's a little confusing.

H2: Can we get to the trail from here?

H1: Well, you could turn around and go back. Or, you can just keep going. This trail crosses the Windy Lake Trail.

H2: So we can just stay on this trail?

H1: Yes, follow the trail for about a mile. Go toward the lake.You'll see a sign for the Windy Lake Trail just before the lake.

H3: Thank you very much.

H1: No problem. Enjoy your hike.

8b-c

I = Interviewer, RC = Dr. Raul Calvi

I: Hello. Our guest today is Dr. Raul Calvi, a scientist who studies animal intelligence. Tell us, Dr. Calvi, is this a new area of research?

RC: Well, historically, a lot of the focus was on trying to teach animals—mostly chimpanzees—language. There were some famous studies in the 1970s...

I: Can you tell us about one?

RC: Sure. One of the most famous studies was with a chimp named Washoe. The chimp had difficulty making sounds, so researchers taught Washoe sign language.

I: By sign language you mean the language that deaf people use...using their hands to speak?

RC: Yes, that's right. In the end, Washoe learned more than 130 words in sign language.

I: 130 words! That's amazing.

RC: Yes, it surprised a lot of people. More recently there's been work with other animals and language...even birds.... There is an African gray parrot named Alex who has learned to name 40 different objects.

I: 40 objects? That seems like a lot for a bird. Is all the research focused on language learning?

RC: It started that way, but I think nowadays researchers are looking at different ways animals might demonstrate intelligence...

I: For example?

RC: Well, people who work with animals a lot, such as zookeepers and veterinarians, always have stories about clever animals...animals that seem to apply some kind of thinking skills to escape from captivity or get more food or something...these kinds of things demonstrate a different kind of intelligence.

I: And there are always so many personal stories from pet owners too...stories about dogs or cats saving their owner's lives...rescuing someone from a fire or something. When I was a child, my grandmother had a cat that found its way home from 20 miles away. These kinds of things must also suggest intelligence.

RC: Yes, that's right. And researchers are now looking at these kinds of personal stories, too.

I: Well, there seems to be a lot of research for scientists studying animal intelligence...

RC: Yes. It's all very exciting...

11b-c

Hello, welcome to our volunteer training session.
First, could you all please check your names off the list? And then take a name tag.
Let's talk a little about why you want to work with animals. Kenny, can you begin?

OK, take a 10-minute break.

OK, let's walk around the zoo. Please don't touch the animals right now. And, of course, do not feed them unless you are instructed to.

UNIT 12

4a-b

A = Alicia, R = Ryan, L = Larry, C = Cassie, M = Mitch

A: Good Morning. I'm Alicia Guerrero. Welcome to our show. Today we're talking about work.... Ryan and I will take your questions.... Caller one is Larry. Hello, Larry?

L: Hi. My question is about personal e-mail at work. I don't have a computer at home, but I use one at work. The problem is that one friend keeps sending me personal e-mail at work. I've told him not to, but he does it anyway. My boss doesn't know, but I don't think she'd like it if she did.

A: Well, obviously your friend doesn't have enough work to do! Seriously, though Larry, I think you're right that this could be a problem. Some bosses don't mind it, but I know a lot of bosses who do. I'd tell your friend very firmly to stop sending e-mail. I'm sure he wouldn't want you to get fired.

R: I agree, but if I were you, I'd also take the initiative and talk to my boss. I'd tell her what happened and apologize. The thing is that I wouldn't want my boss to find out some other way and then think that I was trying to hide something.

A: OK, Larry?

L: Yes, thank you.

R: Our next caller is Cassie. Hello, Cassie?

C: Hi. I work in a big office and I absolutely love my job…except for one thing…. It seems like my co-workers are always saying negative things about our colleagues…and even about our boss. This kind of gossip makes me uncomfortable. I don't think it's good for the atmosphere, not to mention that I'd feel terrible if our boss found out that people were talking about him. It just doesn't seem very nice.

R: Hmm, that is a nasty problem. And even worse, there's not a lot you can do to stop it. I'd suggest you try to stay out of it as much as possible. Keep quiet or, better yet, just leave if you're not comfortable with the topic of discussion.

A: I agree. But I'd also say…if you actually wanted to try and do something about the problem, you could explain how you feel…tell the people talking that you're not comfortable with the gossip…but that might be too direct for some people.

C: Hmm, I'm not sure. I'll think about it. Thank you.

A: And caller 3 is Mitch. Hi, Mitch.

M: Hi. I have a good job, but I'm frustrated because of the owner's son. He started about six months ago…he didn't have any experience and it was clear that he only got the job because of who he was…he didn't even have an interview…it wouldn't be so bad except that he's terrible at his job, so the rest of us have to do most of his work for him…and the worst part is that we all know he gets paid more than we do! Is there anything we can do?

A: Ouch, the boss's family! I don't think there's much you can do about this one, Mitch. Let's face it, the owner of a company can do what he or she wants…even if it's not in the best interest of the company…it doesn't seem like he's going to fire him, does it?

R: Yes, I agree. If you want to keep your job, I think you'll just have to realize that the boss isn't going to fire his own son. Otherwise, you might want to start looking for another job. Either way, it's not an easy situation. Good luck.

M: Thanks.

12a-b

1

A: Let me give you my card.

B: Oh, yes.

A: It has my work phone number and my e-mail address on it. Please contact me any time.

B: Thank you. I will. Here's my card, too. I'll be in touch.

A: OK. It was very nice to meet you. Have a good trip back.

B: Thanks. It was nice to meet you, too. Goodbye.

A: Goodbye.

2

A: Would you be able to mail this out today, please?

B: OK, but I'm not sure I can make it before the mail room closes.

A: I'd really appreciate it if you could try.

B: I'll see what I can do.

A: Thank you.

3

A: We'd like you to have this gift.

B: How nice! Thank you.

C: Thank you. We really appreciate all your hard work.

B: I'm glad. It's my pleasure.

Text Acknowledgments

The publishers are grateful to the individuals and institutions named below for permission to include their materials in this book.

pp. 1, 4: "Frequently Asked Questions" and "South Pole Journal" used by permission of Nathan Tift. Information found on the web site http://nathantift.com/southpole/.

p. 9: "Virtually flirting with love's language" by David Cohen. © Telegraph Group Limited (2001).

p. 13: Adapted from the article "For Some, Pain is Orange" by Susan Hornik. Originally appeared in SMITHSONIAN (February 2001).

p. 23: Based on information from the article "TV Addiction Is No Mere Metaphor," by Robert Kubey and Mihaly Csikzentmihalyi, Scientific American (February 2002).

p. 23: "Why kids are smarter than you" by Carolyn Abraham (January 2001). Reprinted with permission from The Globe and Mail.

p. 29: "A Memory Artist" by Michael Pearce, Exploratorium Magazine: Memory. Vol. 12 No. 2, Summer 1998. © Exploratorium, www.exploratorium.edu.

p. 32: "Memory champ lives by Post-its" by Arlene Levinson (2/1999). Reprinted with permission of The Associated Press.

p. 34: "A is for Apple" used by permission. Exploratorium Magazine: Memory. Vol. 12 No. 2, Summer 1998. © Exploratorium, www.exploratorium.edu.

p. 35: Information about Willie Nelson's Martin guitar found on the web site www.martinguitar.com/artists/famous.php?id=36.

p. 43: Text adapted from "The 19 Kinds of Friends" by Jeremiah Creedon (Utne Reader, Sept/Oct 2001).

p. 46: FRIENDS, by Buzzy Linhart and Mark Klingman © 1971 (Renewed) EMI Unart Catalog Inc. and Kama Sutra Music
All Rights administered by EMI Unart Catalog Inc.
All Rights Reserved   Used by Permission
WARNER BROS. PUBLICATIONS U.S. INC., Miami, FL 33014

p. 48: Adapted information on handwriting analysis. Used by permission of Bart Baggett. © 2002 by HandwritingUniversity.com.

p. 49: "Embrace Your Eccentricity" used by permission of Stephen Tunney (February 2001).

p. 55: "Miss McCarty Goes to Washington" news release originally released 9/21/95 and may be found online at www.pr.usm.edu/oolawash.html. Used by permission of the Department of Marketing and Public Relations at The University of Southern Mississippi, Hattiesburg, MS.

OXFORD
UNIVERSITY PRESS

198 Madison Avenue
New York, NY 10016 USA

Great Clarendon Street
Oxford OX2 6DP England

Oxford   New York
Auckland Bangkok Buenos Aires Cape Town Chennai
Dar es Salaam Delhi Hong Kong Istanbul Karachi Kolkata
Kuala Lumpur Madrid Melbourne Mexico City Mumbai Nairobi
São Paulo Shanghai Taipei Tokyo Toronto

OXFORD is a trademark of Oxford University Press.

ISBN 0-19-453679-3

Copyright © 2004 Oxford University Press

Library of Congress Cataloging-in-Publication Data

Naber, Therese.
  English knowhow. Student book 2 / Therese Naber, Angela Blackwell ;
with Gregory J. Manin.
      p. cm.
  ISBN 0-19-453679-3 (pbk.)
  1. English language—Textbooks for foreign speakers. I. Title:
English knowhow student book 2. II. Blackwell, Angela III. Manin, Gregory
J. IV. Title.
  PE1128 .N237 2004
  428.2'4—dc22

                              2003069131

Editorial Manager: Judith A. Cunningham
Editor: Margaret Brooks
Associate Editor: Carol Balistreri
Assistant Editor: Melinda M. Beck, Alexis Vega-Singer
Design Project Manager: Maria Epes
Senior Designer: Claudia Carlson
Art Editors: Judi DeSouter, Justine Eun
Production Manager: Shanta Persaud
Production Controller: Eve Wong

Printing (last digit): 10 9 8 7 6 5 4 3 2 1

Printed in Hong Kong.

Acknowledgments

Cover photographs: Geri Engberg (woman with book); International Stock/ImageState
(airport); Larry Lawfer/Index Stock (woman on phone); PictureArts Corporation (trophy)

Illustrations: Barbara Bastian pp. 1 (article), 9 (article), 13 (article, abcdef), 17 (credits,
listings), 22 (info sheet), 29 (article), 33 (names), 43 (article), 53 (lottery), 54
(cookies), 63 (cooking words, recipes), 67 (article), 73 (review, excerpt), 82 (song);
Kathy Baxendale pp. 48 (handwriting samples), 59 (list, notice); Annie Bissett pp. 4
(FAQs), 12 (note paper), 23 (articles), 34 (Taking a Trip), 46 (song), 49 (article); Paul
Casale p. 19 (people); Lyndall Culbertson pp. 8 (notepad), 16 (questionnaire, notepad),
18 (list), 19 (survey), 30 (notepad), 35 (article), 39 (diagram), 42 (notepad), 50
(notepad), 55 (article), 61 (quiz), 69 (song), 89 (intro, article), 95 (problems, advice),
97 (question); Ken Dewar p. 18 (desk), 37 (stereo, ring, basket, watch, motorcycle);
Patrick Faricy pp. 56 (restaurant, bank), 91 (hikers); Linda Fong pp. 76 (brochures), 99
(game board); Martha Gavin p. 5 (chores); Paul Hampson p. 11 (cartoons), 24 (TV),
106 & 109 (girl); Rob Hefferan pp. 38 (people), 45 (people); Uldis Klavins pp. 38 (can
opener, scissors, knife, hammer), 53 (tip), 60 (park, clues), 90 (prepositions), 91 (map);
Arnie Levin pp. 21 (man), 94 (cartoon); Laura Hartman Maestro p. 63 (onion, apple,
pan, pot, oven, bowl, grill, pie, salad); Minot-Hershman Studios pp. 9 (messages), 20
(review), 34 (A is for apple), 41 (article), 47 (personality tests), 60 (flyer, chest, trophy),
64 (facts), 90 (diagram, description), 100 (article); Vilma Ortiz-Dillon p. 65 (gift,
wedding); Roger Penwill p. 98 (cartoon); Gary Pierazzi pp. 34 (soap, newspaper,
cookies), 100 (coaster, trash, flowers, mailbox); Angelo Tillery p. 58 (people), 84
(people), 101 (people); Eric Velasquez p. 85 (office, car); Stefano Vitale p. 64 (legend);
Fred Willingham pp. 71 (lost), 93 (people); Paul Zwolak pp. 14 (dancer), 82 (musicians)

Commissioned photographs: Stephen Ogilvy pp. 12 (people), 33 (women), 35 (header),
39 (toaster, microwave, people), 81 (tiger), 102 (people with gift)

*The publishers would like to thank the following for their permission to reproduce
photographs:* ABPL/HINDE, GERALD/Animals Animals/Earth Scenes p. 87 (header);
Garry Adams/Index Stock p. 53 (header); Peter Adams/Getty Images p. 110 (rocks);
Mark Andersen/Rubberball Productions/PictureQuest p. 7 (pool); AP Photo/Tina
Fineberg p. 32 (girl); Joe Atlas/Brand X Pictures/PictureQuest p. 39 (hair dryer); Paul
Barton/CORBIS p. 23 (energetic); Jill Bauerle p.17 (woman at desk); Peter Beck/CORBIS
p. 108 (woman); Bon Color Photo Agency/ImageState p. 36 (T-shirt); Judith Bourque -
www.therealpatchadams.com p. 49 (clown); Brand X Pictures p. 61 (chocolate,

grapefruit, grapes, soda); Brand X Pictures/Alamy pp. 69 (header), 72 (airport), 79
(header); Bristol Museums and Art Gallery p. 75 (on horseback); Phil Buck/Simon and
Schuster p. 73 (book cover); C Squared Studios/Photodisc p. 61 (pasta); CALVIN AND
HOBBES 1992 Watterson. Reprinted with permission of UNIVERSAL PRESS
SYNDICATE. All rights reserved p. 7 (cartoon); Claudia Carlson p. 17 (valley); David
Carriere/Index Stock p. 87 (waterfall); Ken Chernus/Getty Images p. 25 (people); China
Tourism Press/Getty Images p. 97 (woman); Courtesy of Chrysalis Books p. 31 (new city);
Steve Cole/Photodisc/PictureQuest p. 36 (ring); Collection of The New-York Historical
Society/1030 p. 31 (old city); Comstock images pp. 36 (hanger), 39 (coffee maker,
TV remote); Kris Coppieters/SuperStock p. 43 (skydivers); Creatas/PictureQuest p. 36
(guitar); Cumulus p. 61 (header), 100 (flowers); Mel Curtis/Getty Images p. 1
(man on steps); James Darell/Photodisc/PictureQuest p. 9 (girl); David Noton
Photography/Alamy p. 87 (desert); Franco Devilliers/Alamy p. 72 (hotel);
DigitalVision/PictureQuest p. 27 (move in); elektraVision/Index Stock p. 43
(header); Nicholas Eveleigh/SuperStock p. 39 (DVD player); Exploratorium,
www.exploratorium.edu p. 29 (photo); Najlah Feanny/CORBIS p. 92 (chimp); Jon
Feingersh/CORBIS p. 23 (relaxed); Dennis Galante/CORBIS p. 37 ("Mauricio"); Chris
George/CORBIS p. 49 (gnomes); Goodcomm/Alamy p. 1 (playing guitar); Jeff
Greenberg/age fotostock p. 92 (dolphin); Jeff Greenberg/Index Stock p. 1 (beach); Peter
Holmes/age fotostock p. 61 (tea); Jason Homa/Getty Images p. 83 (woman on right);
Dave G. Houser/CORBIS p. 69 (van); Richard Hutchings/CORBIS p. 7 (birthday);
ImageState/Alamy p. 27 (party); InternationalStock/ImageState p. 79 (baseball); "IT
COULD HAPPEN TO YOU" ©1994 Columbia TriStar Pictures. All Rights Reserved
Courtesy of TriStar Pictures p. 53 (poster); Chase Jarvis/Photodisc/PictureQuest p. 27
(skiing); Buddy Jenssen/Index Stock p. 36 (coin); J.C. Kanny/LORPRESSE/CORBIS p.
36 (necklace); Cheryl Johnson p. 17 (movie set); Ronnie Kaufman/CORBIS p. 1
(header); Photos courtesy of Kenji Kawakami/Sakai Agency pp. 40 (Chindogu photos),
41 (Chindogu photos); key Color/Index Stock Images/PictureQuest p. 67 (woman);
Helen King/CORBIS p. 2 (gym); Howard Kingsnorth/Getty Images p. 70 (woman);
Douglas Kirkland/CORBIS p. 22 (movie set); Carol Kohen/Getty Images p. 95 (header);
Bob Krist/CORBIS p. 30 (garden); Lucidio Studio Inc./CORBIS p. 17 (TV); John
Lund/Getty Images p. 103 (lightning); Robert Mankoff/CartoonBank p. 51 (cartoon);
James McLoughlin/age fotostock p. 46 (people); Ryan McVay/Photodisc pp. 5 (friends),
61 (fork); Ryan McVay/Photodisc/PictureQuest p. 102 (envelope); MPTV.net p. 20
(poster); Kathryn L. O'Dell p. 110 (salt flat); Stuart Pearce/age fotostock p. 9 (header);
Jules Perrier/CORBIS p. 57 (man); Richard Pharoah/ImageState p. 36 (window); Photo
24/Brand X Pictures/PictureQuest p. 81 (street); PhotoLink/Photodisc/PictureQuest p.
79 (hockey); Photonica p. 27 (header); Philippe Poulet/Mission/Getty Images p. 75
(modern woman); Chris Rainier/CORBIS p. 70 (hitchhiker); Vittoriano Rastelli/CORBIS
p. 68 (model); Stephanie Rausser/Taxi/Getty Images p. 88 (garden); Anthony
Redpath/CORBIS p. 107 (man); Reuters New Media Inc./CORBIS p. 35 (man); Rick
Rickman p. 89 (man); John A. Rizzo/Photodisc/PictureQuest p. 61 (lemonade); Phillipe
Roy/Alamy p. 68 (grapes); Royalty-Free/CORBIS pp. 37 (couple, "Bruce"), 87 (island);
RubberBall Productions/Getty Images p. 83 (man); RubberBallProductions/PictureQuest
p. 37 ("Elaine, Mia"); Roberto Santos/Index Stock p. 16 (bread); Scala/ArtResource, NY
p. 88 (painting); Ariel Skelley/CORBIS p. 108 (man); Steve Smith/SuperStock p. 43
(women); Joe Sohm/PictureQuest p. 79 (rodeo); Stock Image Rendezvous/ImageState
p. 79 (golf); Stockbyte/PictureQuest p. 95 (men); Stockbyte/PictureQuest p. 95 (men);
StockImage/ImageState p. 44 (people); ThinkStock/Index Stock p. 77 (man); Mark
Turner/age fotostock p. 87 (mountain); Photos Courtesy of the University of
Mississippi p. 55 (Oseola McCarty); Phillip Van Den Berg/age fotostock p. 67
(ostriches); Tom Wagner/CORBIS SABA p. 64 (cooking), 68 (cars); John Ward -
www.johnwardinventor.co.uk p. 49 (podmobile); Simon Watson/Getty Images p. 102
(cards); Jim Weems p. 95 (book cover); Ross Whitaker/Getty Images p. 7 (wash car);
Chaloner Woods/Hulton Archive/Getty Images p. 83 (woman on left); Michael S.
Yamashita/CORBIS p. 109 (city).

Special thanks to: Nathan Tift pp. 1 (slushies), 3 (photo), 4 (photo); Calum Richards,
George Richards, and Paula Rubino p. 7 (being a child); Gláucia Arruda, Anna
Berezowski, and Selma Trus p. 11 (favorite words); Jennifer Katz p. 17 (interview); Lori
Parins p. 21 (TV extra); Franco Magnani p. 29 (painting, picture of self); Helen Monson
O'Dell p. 31 (photo, painting especially painted for *English KnowHow*); Lisa Lacher p.
57 (barter experience); Herr's Potato Chips p.62 (potato chip factory information and
photo); Carol Balistreri, Liz Kennedy, and Mary Martin p. 70 (travel experiences);
Michele Hament p. 81 (parking tiger);

*The authors and publishers extend thanks to the following English Language Teaching
professionals and institutions for their invaluable support and feedback during the
development of this series:* Gill Adams (Brazil); Virgílio Almeida and staff (Brazil);
Barbara Bangle (Mexico); Jocélia Pizzamiglio Basso and staff (Brazil); Vera Berk (Brazil);
James Boyd (Japan); Bonnie Brown de Masis (Costa Rica); Janaína Cardoso and staff
(Brazil); Hector Castillo (Mexico); Dr. Robin Chapman (Japan); Ana Isabel Delgado
(Brazil); Nora Díaz (Mexico); Maria da Graça Duarte and staff (Brazil); Stephen
Edmunds (Mexico); Israel Escalante (Mexico); Raquel Faria and staff (Brazil); Verónica
Galván (Mexico); Saul Santos García (Mexico); Carmen Gehrke and staff (Brazil); Arlete
Würschig Gonçalves and staff (Brazil); Kimberley Humphries (Mexico); Michelle
Johnstone (Canada); Sonya Kozicki-Jones (Costa Rica); Jean-Pierre Louvrier (Brazil);
Shan-jen Amy Lu (Taiwan); Mary Meyer (Paraguay); Dulce Montes de Oca (Mexico);
Harold Murillo (Colombia); Connie Reyes (Mexico); Carmen Oliveira and staff (Brazil);
Joselanda de Oliveira and staff (Brazil); Thelma Félix Oliveira (Brazil); Ane Cibele
Palma and staff (Brazil); Eliane Cunha Peixoto and staff (Brazil); Verónica Olguín
(Mexico); Claudia Otake (Mexico); Nicola Sarjeant (Korea); Débora Schisler and staff
(Brazil); Lilian Munhoz Soares and staff (Brazil); Sharon Springer (Costa Rica); Sílvia
Thalacker and staff (Brazil); Kris Vicca (Taiwan); Ignacio Yepes and staff (Mexico);
Daniel Zarate (Mexico); Mirna Züge (Brazil).
Centro Cultural Brasil-Estados Unidos, Santos; Centro de Línguas Estrangeiras
Mackenzie, São Paulo; ENEP Acatlán, Edo. de México; English Forever, Salvador; Escola
Técnica Estadual Fernando Prestes, Sorocaba; GreenSystem, Belo Horizonte; IBEU,
Fortaleza; IBEU, Rio; Instituto Cultural Brasileiro Norte-Americano, Porto Alegre;
Interamericano-CCBEU, Curitiba; MAI, Belo Horizonte; Plus!, Brasília; Quatrum, Porto
Alegre; SENAC, Rio; Seven, São Paulo; Talkative, São Paulo; Universidad Autónoma de
México; Universidad Autónoma del Estado de México; Universidade Católica de
Brasília; Universidade de Caxias do Sul-PLE; Universidad La Salle, León, Guanajuato;
Universidad Latino Americano, Mexico City; Universidad Nacional Autónoma de
México; Universidad Autónoma de Guadalajara.